PRACTICAL ORCHESTRATION

THE CHICAGO SYMPHONY ORCHESTRA
FREDERICK A. STOCK, CONDUCTOR

Practical Orchestration

By
ARTHUR OLAF ANDERSEN

Author of "First Forty Lessons in Harmony;" "Second Forty Lessons in Harmony;"
"Strict and Free Counterpoint;" "Essentials of Musical Form"

WITH SAILS & OARS

Price $3.50

C. C. BIRCHARD & COMPANY
BOSTON

CONTENTS

PAGE

CHAPTER I. THE VIOLIN 13
Fingering in First Position. Diagram of Finger Board. Names of Dif-
ferent Parts of Instrument. Exercises. Examples of First Position
Technic.

CHAPTER II. THE VIOLIN 18
Double-Stops in First Position. Different Varieties of Bowing. Second
and Third Positions. Examples and Exercises.

CHAPTER III. THE VIOLIN 25
Double-Stops in Second and Third Positions. Fourth, Fifth and Remain-
ing Positions. Natural and Artificial Harmonics. Examples and
Exercises.

CHAPTER IV. THE VIOLIN 33
Triple-Stops and Quadruple-Stops. Tremolo-Staccato and Tremolo-Legato
and Other Manners of using the Bow. Examples. Exercises in the
Combining of Two, Three and Four Violins.

CHAPTER V. THE VIOLA 41
Fingering of First and Third Positions. Diagram of Finger Board. Double-
Stops in Both Positions. Bowing. Examples. Exercises in Com-
bination with Violins.

CHAPTER VI. THE VIOLA 47
Remaining Positions. Triple-Stops and Quadruple-Stops. Natural and
Artificial Harmonics. Character of Tone-Color in Conjunction with
Violins. Exercises.
THE VIOLA D'AMORE 52
Examples.

CHAPTER VII. THE VIOLONCELLO 55
First Position. Diagram showing Fingering. Double-Stops. Bowing.
Examples. Exercises in Combination with Violins and Viola.

CHAPTER VIII. THE VIOLONCELLO 61
Triple-Stops and Quadruple-Stops. Natural and Artificial Harmonics.
String Trio and Quartet. Examples. Exercises in Combining the
Violin, Viola and Cello.

CHAPTER IX. THE DOUBLE-BASS (CONTRABASS) 66
Fingering, Bowing and Harmonics. Examples. Exercises.

CHAPTER X. THE STRING ORCHESTRA 79
Examples and Exercises.

CHAPTER XI. THE FLUTE 91
Range, Technic, Combinations with the Strings. Examples and Exercises.
THE PICCOLO 92
THE BASS-FLUTE 98

CONTENTS

PAGE

CHAPTER XII. THE OBOE 99
    Range, Technic, Tone-Color and Combinations. Examples and Exercises.
THE ENGLISH HORN 102
    Range, Tone-Color and Combinations. Examples. Exercises.

CHAPTER XIII. THE CLARINET 105
    Range, Technic, Tone-Color, Uses and Character. Examples and Exercises.
THE Eb CLARINET 113

CHAPTER XIV. THE BASS CLARINET 114

CHAPTER XV. THE BASSOON 117
    Tone-Color, Technic and Combinations. Examples and Exercises.
THE DOUBLE-BASSOON 121
THE STRINGS AND WOOD-WINDS 123

CHAPTER XVI. THE HUNTING-HORN 127
THE FRENCH HORN 128
    Range, Technic, Tone-Color, Uses and Combinations. Examples. Exercises.

CHAPTER XVII. THE VALVE TRUMPET 139
    Range and Technic. Tone-Color, Uses and Combinations. Examples and Exercises.
THE BASS TRUMPET 143
THE CORNET 144

CHAPTER XVIII. THE TROMBONES 146
    Range, Technic, Pedal-Tones and Combinations with Other Instruments. Examples. Exercises.
THE BASS TROMBONE 148

CHAPTER XIX. THE TUBA 153
    Range, Technic and Uses. Examples. Exercises.

CHAPTER XX. THE SAXOPHONE FAMILY 158
THE SARRUSOPHONE 159

CHAPTER XXI. THE HARP 161

CHAPTER XXII. THE PERCUSSION INSTRUMENTS . . . 169
TUNED PERCUSSIONS:
    The Kettledrums 170
    The Chromatic Drums 171
    Cathedral Chimes 173
    Orchestra Bells 173
    Celesta 175
    The Xylophone 177
    The Marimba 178
THE UNTUNED PERCUSSIONS:
    The Snare Drum 178
    The Bass Drum 181
    The Tambourine 183

CONTENTS

PAGE

CHAPTER XXII. THE PERCUSSION INSTRUMENTS — *Con.*
THE UNTUNED PERCUSSIONS — *Con.*
    The Triangle 185
    The Cymbals 187
    The Gong or Tam-tam 189
    The Castanets 189

CHAPTER XXIII. THE TENOR BANJO 191
  THE MANDOLIN 192
  THE GUITAR 194
  THE CIMBALON 195

CHAPTER XXIV. COMBINATION OF STRINGS, WOOD-WINDS, BRASSES AND PER-
       CUSSIONS 196

CHAPTER XXV. SUGGESTIONS FOR COPYING ORCHESTRAL PARTS 201

CHAPTER XXVI. MUSICAL TERMS, EXPRESSIONS AND INDICATIONS USED BY OR-
       CHESTRAL COMPOSERS 204

EXAMPLES FROM VARIOUS SCORES 214–245

ALPHABETICAL INDEX 246

ILLUSTRATIONS

The Chicago Symphony Orchestra .... Frontispiece
Back View of a Stradivarius .... Facing 14
Banjo Finger Board with Viola Tuning .... Page 193
Barrère Ensemble .... Facing 360
Bass Drum 181
Bass Drum Stick 181
Bassoon, The 77
Bells, Orchestra 177
Castanets, Orchestra ....
Cello Finger Board .... Page 20
Chimes, Cathedral .... Facing 179
Clarinet Family, The 205
Cornet, The B Flat or A 136
Cymbals, The 177
Double Bass or Contrabass 66
English Horn, The 90
Euphonium, The B Flat Five-Keyed 155
Euphonium, The B Flat Four-Keyed 154
Flutes, Wooden and Metal 81
French Horn, The 198
Front View of a Stradivarius 15
Gong 177
Guitar, The 181
Harp, The Double-Action 101
Harp Pedals .... Page 261
Kettledrums, Chromatic .... Facing 171
Kettledrums, Old-Style 185
Mandolin, The 194
Marimba, The 275
Oboe, The 90
Piccolos, Woody and Metal 97
Plectrums 191
Sarrusophone 180
Saxophone, B Flat Bass 158
Saxophone, C Melody Tenor 158
Saxophone Family, The 159
Snare Drum 191
Tambourine, The 177
Tenor Banjo, The 191
Triangle, The 177
Trombone, The 148
Trumpet, The B Flat or A 139

ILLUSTRATIONS

The Chicago Symphony Orchestra . . . . *Frontispiece*
Back View of a Stradivarius . . . . *Facing* 14
Banjo Finger Board with Viola Tuning . . . . *Page* 193
Barrère Ensemble . . . . *Facing* 200
Bass Drum . . . . " 181
Bass Drum Stick . . . . " 181
Bassoon, The . . . . " 117
Bells, Orchestra . . . . " 177
Castanets, Orchestra . . . . " 177
Cello Finger Board . . . . *Page* 56
Chimes, Cathedral . . . . *Facing* 173
Clarinet Family, The . . . . " 105
Cornet, The B Flat or A . . . . " 139
Cymbals, The . . . . " 177
Double-Bass or Contrabass . . . . " 66
English Horn, The . . . . " 99
Euphonium, The B Flat Five-Keyed . . . . " 153
Euphonium, The B Flat Four-Keyed . . . . " 154
Flutes, Wooden and Metal . . . . " 91
French Horn, The . . . . " 128
Front View of a Stradivarius . . . . " 13
Gong . . . . " 177
Guitar, The . . . . " 194
Harp, The Double-Action . . . . " 161
Harp Pedals . . . . *Page* 161
Kettledrums, Chromatic . . . . *Facing* 171
Kettledrums, Old-Style . . . . " 169
Mandolin, The . . . . " 194
Marimba, The . . . . " 173
Oboe, The . . . . " 99
Piccolos, Wooden and Metal . . . . " 91
Plectrums . . . . " 191
Sarrusophone . . . . " 160
Saxophone, B Flat Bass . . . . " 158
Saxophone, C Melody Tenor . . . . " 158
Saxophone Family, The . . . . " 159
Snare Drum . . . . " 181
Tambourine, The . . . . " 177
Tenor Banjo, The . . . . " 191
Triangle, The . . . . " 177
Trombone, The . . . . " 146
Trumpet, The B Flat or A . . . . " 139

ILLUSTRATIONS

Tuba, The Double B Flat	*Facing*	154
Tuba, The E Flat	"	153
Viola Finger Board	*Page*	43
Violin Finger Board, First Position	"	15
Violin Finger Board, Second Position	"	19
Violin Finger Board, Third Position	"	20
Violin Finger Board, Fourth Position	"	27
Violin Finger Board, Fifth Position	"	28
Violoncello, The	*Facing*	55
Violoncello, Back	"	56
Xylophone, The	"	177

ILLUSTRATIONS FROM SCORES

Concert Overture in C Major (with Organ)	Arthur Edward Johnstone	214
Comes Autumn Time	Leo Sowerby	215
C Minor Symphony	Frederick A. Stock	217
Danse de la Balerine	Strawinsky	240
Deuxieme Symphonie	d'Indy	216
Dirge from Concerto Grosso	Ernest Bloch	218
Ein Heldenleben	Strauss	244
Flivver Ten Million	Frederick S. Converse	219
Forest Spirits	Edward A. Macdowell	220
Good Friday Spell	Wagner	241
Il Finto Arlecchino	G. Francesco Malipiero	221
In Bohemia	Henry Hadley	222
Irish Rhapsody	Victor Herbert	223
La Grand Pàque Russe	Rimsky-Korsakow	242
La Mort de Tintaglles	Charles M. Loeffler	224
Legend Symphonique	Ernest Schelling	225
New England Symphony	Edgar Stillman-Kelley	226
New Year's Eve in New York	Werner Janssen	231
Offrandes	Edgar Varèse	227
Overture to a Drama	Arthur Shepherd	228
Pan and the Priest	Howard Hanson	229
Peer Gynt Suite	Edvard Grieg	230
Polonaise	Bach	243
Romantic Suite, A	Max Reger	232
Saturday's Child, Op. 42	Emerson Whithorne	233
Scheherazade	Rimsky-Korsakow	245
Second Symphony	A. Borodin	234
Sinfonietta	G. W. Chadwick	235
Soliloquy	Bernard Rogers	236
Sonata	Pietro Castrucci	239
Volga Boatmen	Stoessel	238
William Tell (Overture)	Rossini	237

INTRODUCTION

This book on "Practical Orchestration" should be considered more in the light of a textbook than as a complete treatise on the subject. Each chapter has a definite assignment of exercises which should be faithfully carried out by the student and carefully corrected and commented upon by the teacher.

As each new instrument appears in the following pages, the student should either arrange suitable piano compositions or compose short sketches characteristic of the workable compass and technic of the new color. This adding of the instruments, one at a time, will familiarize the student with the general ensemble. He should be aiding himself by concentrated study of the scores of well-known orchestral writers. It is not enough for the student to know the range of the instruments and how written; he must also study the color and combinations as well as the juxtapositions with all other orchestral instruments.

The student is advised not to attempt writing ahead of the general instruction contained in each chapter, but rather to adhere strictly to the subject at hand.

Great attention should be given to the exact fingerings of stringed instruments as well as to phrasing and tone-colors in combinations. Wood-winds should be carefully studied, not only as to independence in grouping, but also as to strengthening the other choirs of the orchestra through doublings and filled-in voices. All these points should be particularly noted in studying scores.

The student is advised to read other textbooks on orchestration in order to obtain as much information as possible on the subject. He will find slight deviations in this work, such as differences in range and omission of certain difficulties which no longer exist because of the manufacture of new instruments, as well as the advanced versatility of present-day performers. Certain trills on the oboe, for instance, indicated as impossible in some older textbooks, are to-day made possible through the improvement of this instrument. Other minor details of a similar nature, noted as the student advances, ultimately will increase his freedom of action in orchestral composition.

An occasional informative lesson from exponents of orchestral instruments will be invaluable to the student in his work, and he should take every opportunity which offers of obtaining such knowledge from skilled players. This does not mean, necessarily, that he must be able to play these instruments, but he should learn their possibilities.

THE AUTHOR.

THE VIOLIN

SCROLL

PEGS (EBONY)

PEG BOX

SADDLE OR NUT (EBONY)

FINGER BOARD (EBONY)

PURFLING

BELLY (PINE OR SPRUCE)

BOUTS

SOUND HOLES

BRIDGE

TAIL PIECE (EBONY)

LOWER SADDLE

BUTTON

FRONT VIEW OF A STRADIVARIUS (1740)

On the inside of the violin are found the bass bar to the left of the center; the sound post on the chanterelle or treble side; the twelve lining pieces; the four corner blocks strengthening the bouts: two large blocks, one at either end, to meet the strain of the strings. The sides of the instrument are composed of six parts, and the purfling around the edges of the belly and back is composed of thirty six distinct pieces.

CHAPTER I. THE VIOLIN

Italian: *Violino*
French: *Violon*
German: *Geige* or *Violine*

FINGERING IN FIRST POSITION — DIAGRAM OF FINGER BOARD —
NAMES OF DIFFERENT PARTS OF INSTRUMENT — EXERCISES —
EXAMPLES OF FIRST-POSITION TECHNIC

The violin is constructed of over seventy-five pieces of pine, maple
and ebony. Of these pieces, eight are not built solidly into the instrument,
but are held in place through the tension of the strings and the delicate
adjustment of fitting.

The four strings are tuned in fifths: G, D, A and E, and are made of
catgut, the lowest, G, being wound with thin metal wire, usually silver.

The finger board, over which the strings are stretched, is about eleven
and one-half inches in length, widening slightly as it approaches the bridge.

By placing the first finger firmly on the G string, about an inch above
the nut (see illustration), and pressing it against the finger board, the
whole step above, or A, will result. The second finger pressing the string
against the finger board at approximately the same distance above A will
give B. The third finger being required to play C, in this instance, is pressed
down but half an inch above B, and the fourth finger, a whole inch again,
giving D. This D is the same tone as the next open string, and consequently
can be obtained by using the fourth finger on the G string or by drawing
the bow across the open string.

By repeating the same process of fingering on the D string as was
used on the G string, the first finger will give E, the second finger F♯, the
third finger G, and the fourth finger A.

In fingering the A string (G scale) the half steps will be found between
the first and second fingers. The E string fingering will be identical with
that of the A string. We have thus fingered all the diatonic tones in the
G scale in the first position. If it be desired to produce semi-tones, the
finger is pushed forward for sharps and drawn back for flats.

There are two observations to be taken into consideration in the
fingering of the violin: The first is, always to employ the proper finger for
the proper note. Each finger must be the guardian of three semi-tones.
For instance, the first finger on the G string should take care of A, A♭ and
A♯; the second finger, of B, B♭ and B♯; the third finger, of C, C♭ and C♯;
and the fourth finger, of D, D♭ and D♯. Consequently, as will be seen,

13

each finger must be alert to its required duties and not trespass on the territory of its neighbor's space of action unless the neighboring finger is busily occupied elsewhere and cannot be in two places at the same time. In this case a momentary substitution may take place; but this will rarely be necessary except in double-stopping (playing two tones at the same time), or through enharmonic reading in order to facilitate a smoother technic.

The second observation is in regard to the use of the open strings. Violinists seldom employ the open strings. The open G string is naturally excepted; but otherwise, except in very quick passage work, such as scales, arpeggios and certain violinistic figures, it is preferable to employ the fourth finger rather than an open string. The quality of the tone of the open string is so bright and hard that the difference between it and the stopped tone is very noticeable.

In the case of double flats or double sharps, it is always best to change the note enharmonically and give it the fingering of the note to which the change is made. A, on the G string, while not a perfectly true B♭♭, would be much easier to play quickly than would the B♭♭, and would also be less awkward with the first finger than with the second.

The above illustration shows the fingering of the G scale in the first position.

THE VIOLIN

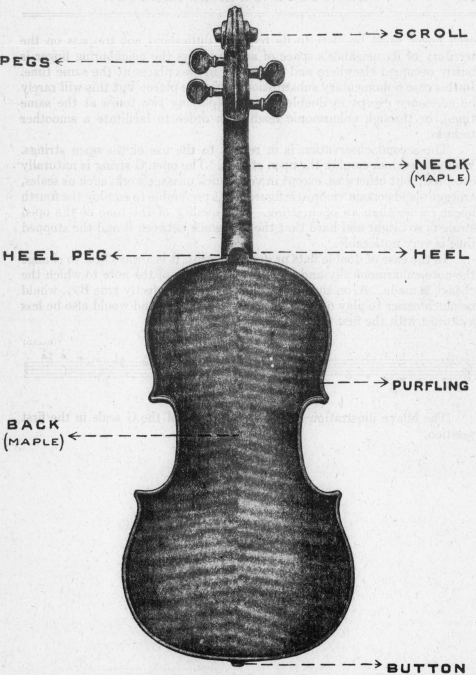

SCROLL

PEGS

NECK
(MAPLE)

HEEL PEG

HEEL

PURFLING

BACK
(MAPLE)

BUTTON

BACK VIEW OF A STRADIVARIUS (1740)

The back of the violin is usually formed of two pieces of maple, although but one piece may be
used. The belly of the violin is generally made of two pieces, although but one may be used; but this
less frequently than in the construction of the back.

FIRST POSITION

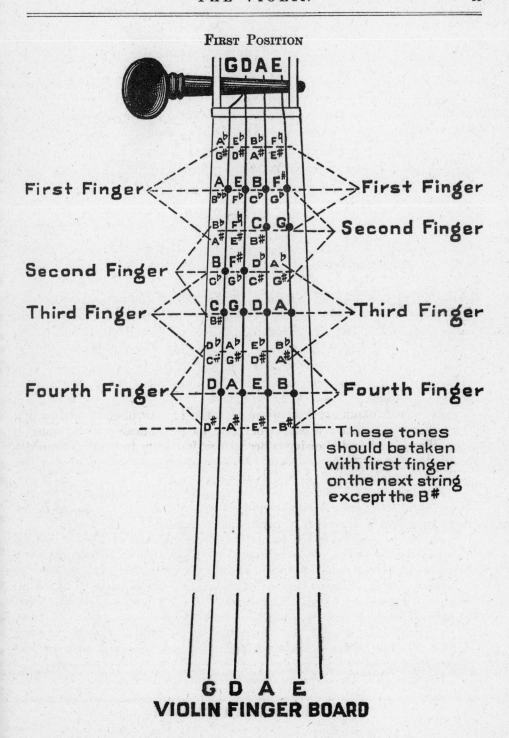

VIOLIN FINGER BOARD

The technic of the violin in the first position is limited to two and a third octaves so far as range is concerned. Otherwise, tone-color in any variety from *ppp* to *fff* can be obtained as well as any degree of speed in the performance of repeated notes, scales, arpeggios and tone figures. Long skips that require jumping the bow to and from the outer strings, or that necessitate awkward back and forth rapid changes of the bow over a middle string, should be avoided when possible.

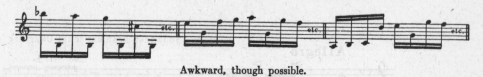

Awkward, though possible.

Passage work, in any degree of velocity, is most effective when written across neighboring strings.

Not difficult.

Chromatic scales are often difficult of distinct intonation, especially if played rapidly, although the slight "cloudiness" that results is not altogether unpleasant.

The student is advised to procure for himself a copy of Mendelssohn's *Songs Without Words* for use as practical illustrations of the various fingerings and bowings necessary for him to master in order to write correctly for the strings. He will also use these *Songs* in practising the various combinations which will be later presented.

His first exercise will not be that of writing an original piece for the violin, but of fingering several compositions already written and proving them according to the chart of the violin finger board.

Exercise I. Finger the melody on the first page of Mendelssohn's *Songs Without Words*, No. 1. Do not forget the signature, for this must be taken into strict consideration. Do not use any open string.

Exercise II. Finger the melody and the accompanying figure of No. 7 on the treble clef to the first repeat bar as though two violins were being employed.

Exercise III. Finger the upper clef of No. 36 as though it were written for two, three or four violins. Use only the last page of the composition.

Exercise IV. Do the same with the first page of No. 39.

EXAMPLES OF FIRST POSITION

Larghetto

César Franck: "D major Quartet"

1st Violin

dolce, molto cantabile

etc.

Allegro

Johannes Brahms: "Fest Overture"

1st Violin

pp

etc.

Lentement

Vincent d'Indy: "Quartet. E major"

1st Violin

mf dim.   pp

etc.

2d Violin

mf   dim.   pp

Light and easy

Fred. Stock: "C minor Quartet"

1st Violin

p   più p

etc.

2d Violin

p   più p

CHAPTER II. THE VIOLIN

Double-Stops in First Position — Different Varieties of Bowing — Second and Third Positions — Examples and Exercises

Double-stopping on the violin is the sounding of two notes simultaneously. This is effected by drawing the bow across two neighboring strings. Double-stops are used a great deal in simple orchestrations, especially for the second violin and viola, and often for the first violin for special effects and cadences. In studying double-stopping in the first position, the chart of the finger board in first position should be followed, and the exact fingering of each double-stop carefully indicated. It will be noted that when two notes are a perfect fifth apart they are directly across the two strings, and but one finger need be used with which to stop them. The student is warned against the use of double-stops in perfect fifths in quick tempo. The fact that one finger must cover two strings at precisely the same point with unhesitating surety might be reflected upon as a cause for their impracticability, and the student will see how any slight wavering of the finger-tip will cause the resultant tones to be out of tune. In moderate or slow tempo, more time in which to gauge exactness of fingering permits of their use. If the two notes are either an augmented fifth or a diminished fifth, a substitution fingering is necessary. This will be noted in the study of the following double-stops in the first position on the G and D strings:

This illustration comprises all the possible double-stops between the G and D strings. Similar tables should be made for the double-stops for the D and A strings, as well as for the A and E strings.

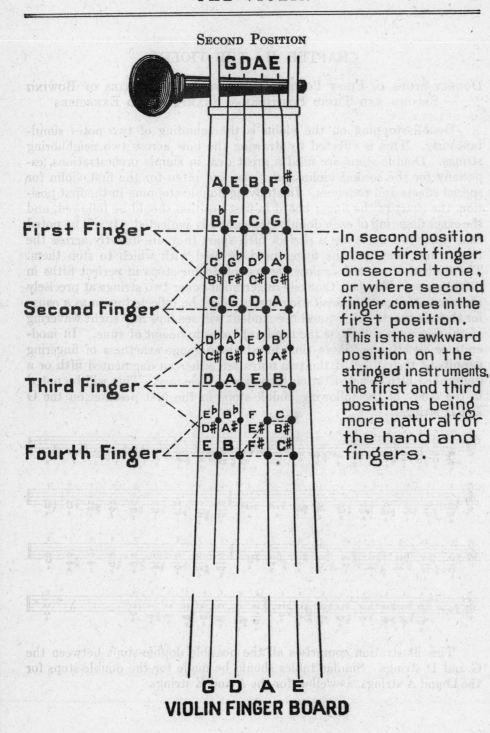

SECOND POSITION

GDAE

First Finger

Second Finger

Third Finger

Fourth Finger

In second position place first finger on second tone, or where second finger comes in the first position. This is the awkward position on the stringed instruments, the first and third positions being more natural for the hand and fingers.

G D A E
VIOLIN FINGER BOARD

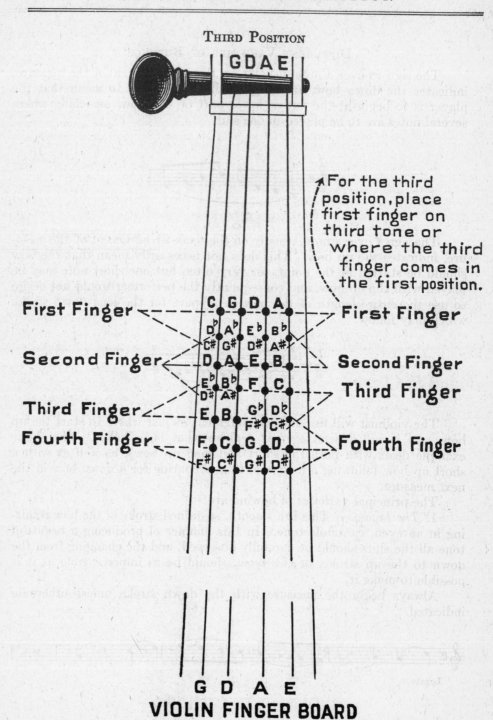

THIRD POSITION

GDAE

For the third position, place first finger on third tone or where the third finger comes in the first position.

First Finger — C G D A — First Finger

Second Finger — D A E B — Second Finger

Third Finger — E B — Third Finger

Fourth Finger — F C G D — Fourth Finger

G D A E
VIOLIN FINGER BOARD

DIFFERENT VARIETIES OF BOWINGS

The sign ⊓ over a note, usually on the strong accent of the measure, indicates the down bow, and is generally understood to mean that the player is to begin at the nut or lower part of the bow, especially where several notes are to be played in one slur.

The sign **V** over a note, usually on the weak or off accent of the measure, indicates the up bow. This does not necessarily mean that the bow should be started at the point, for very often but one short note may be played with the up bow, and consequently the performer would not desire to use the entire length of the bow to prepare for the long down stroke which may follow.

The violinist will use his own judgment of just where to start the up bow, and it will depend a great deal on what is to follow. The above example deals with both the short and long up bows, as well as with a short up bow following a long one, thus preparing for a down bow in the next measure.

The principal varieties of bowing are:

1. *The Legato.* — This is a smooth, sustained stroke of the bow resulting in an even, cantabile tone. In this manner of producing a beautiful tone all the slurs should be carefully observed, and the changing from the down to the up stroke, or *vice versa*, should be as imperceptible as it is possible to make it.

Always begin the measure with the down stroke unless otherwise indicated.

Legato.

2. *The Staccato.* — This is either a short, crisp stroke of the bow or a division of the full bow into short, snappy portions. In staccato bowing the hair of the bow is not supposed to leave the string.

Played at the top of the bow.   Single strokes.

Slurred staccato.

3. *The Spiccato.* — This is the springing bow, the hair leaving the string for each note.

Usually played in the middle of the bow.

4. *The Marcato.* — A firm stroke using about one-third of the bow.

5. *Détaché.* — This is a quick, full stroke of the bow. A sustained evenness of tone should be maintained with both the up and down strokes. There is also a short détaché, using about one-third of the bow, preferably at the top.

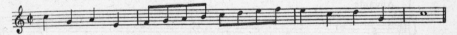

Accentuated bowing, indicating a firm, strong stroke of the bow for each tone, is indicated by the sign > over the notes.

Use from one-half to two-thirds of the bow for each stroke, according to the time value of the note.

There are many combinations of bowings, all more or less variations of the legato, staccato, spiccato and marcato, which will be taken up in another chapter.

Exercise I. Double-stop the last thirteen measures of Mendelssohn's *Songs*, No. 47. Use only one violin for the notes on the treble clef. Where a double-stop is not possible, use only the melody note, but finger every note in the passage, indicating the nature of the bowing to be employed.

Exercise II. Use two violins for this exercise. The problem is to select the best notes for double-stopping in the first sixteen measures of No. 48. As the three upper voices are to be considered, there will be but one double-stop possible on one or the other violin at the same time. Consequently the division of the double-stopping and single-stopping must be seriously considered from the viewpoint of smoothness. In the choice of intervals to be used for the double-stops, it is well to remember that major and minor sixths and major and minor thirds, augmented fourths and diminished fifths are preferable when possible, but that all other intervals may be employed. All these exercises should be properly bowed.

EXAMPLE

Exercise III. Arrange the first twelve measures of No. 47 for three violins.

Exercise IV. Transpose the first eight measures of No. 22 an octave higher and finger the melody in the third position.

EXAMPLES OF THIRD POSITION TECHNIC AND DOUBLE-STOPS

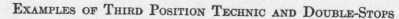

Easy double stops in 1st position.

Helen Dallam: "Father Neptune Smiles"

Adagio

Earnest Walker: "Fantasia in D"

Tempo di Mazurka

Helen Dallam: "Mazurka"

1st Position — 2d Position - - - - - 3d Position - - - - -

Moderato

1st Position

Allegretto

W. F. Ambrosio: "Tell me, Mother"

Violin

CHAPTER III. THE VIOLIN

DOUBLE-STOPS IN SECOND AND THIRD POSITIONS — FOURTH, FIFTH AND REMAINING POSITIONS — NATURAL AND ARTIFICIAL HARMONICS — EXAMPLES AND EXERCISES

Double-stops in the second position are not as frequently employed as are those of the first and third positions. They should be written carefully and fingered, as a proper knowledge of them is essential in orchestration.

The double-stops on the G and D strings in the second position, as shown in the above illustration, are nearly all possible in the first position and are more practicable in that position, but those indicated thus, *, are playable in the second or third position only, and then preferably in the third.

In order to have a thoroughly comprehensive knowledge of the violin, the student of orchestration should study these double-stops very carefully, and also should write the double-stops on the D and A strings as well as on the A and E strings, indicating those which are not possible in the first position.

Not only is it essential to know the second position double-stops, but the use of the second position for melody, playing in keys of four, five and six sharps, as well as four, five and six flats, should be carefully studied. Formerly, the composers showed great consideration for the orchestra performers by being very careful to select only such keys as best suited the fluent technic of the strings and the transposing instruments. As an example, take Beethoven's nine symphonies as to keys:

Symphony No. 1, C major.
Symphony No. 2, D major.
Symphony No. 3 (Eroica), E♭ major.
Symphony No. 4, B♭ major.
Symphony No. 5, C minor.
Symphony No. 6 (Pastoral), F major.

Symphony No. 7, A major.
Symphony No. 8, F major.
Symphony No. 9 (Choral), D minor.

It will be noted that keys of more than three sharps or three flats were avoided, although, during the course of such works, modulations to keys of still more sharps or flats than appear in the original signatures were bound to occur.   But in these days, technical proficiency in orchestral performance having greatly advanced, it is not uncommon to find music in four, five and even six sharps or flats.   Such music, while inclined to be awkward in the easy positions of the stringed instruments, is more often than not quite easy in the so-called awkward positions.

Double-stops in the third position are easier of performance than are those in the second position, but are more difficult than those of the first position.

The double-stops indicated thus, *, are playable only in the third position.   The other stops are not difficult in the first position.   The double-stops on the D and A strings, as well as those on the A and E strings, should be carefully written and fingered.

Of the remaining positions, sixth, seventh, eighth, ninth, etc., it is urged that the student make charts of the fingering but not of the double-stops, as these, except for solo purposes, are impracticable.   For further work he should study the violin parts of all scores obtainable, noting the bowing indicated as well as observing the double-stopping, and whenever opportunity offers he should follow the scores at actual performances of the music, thereby deriving confidence in his own efforts.

FOURTH POSITION

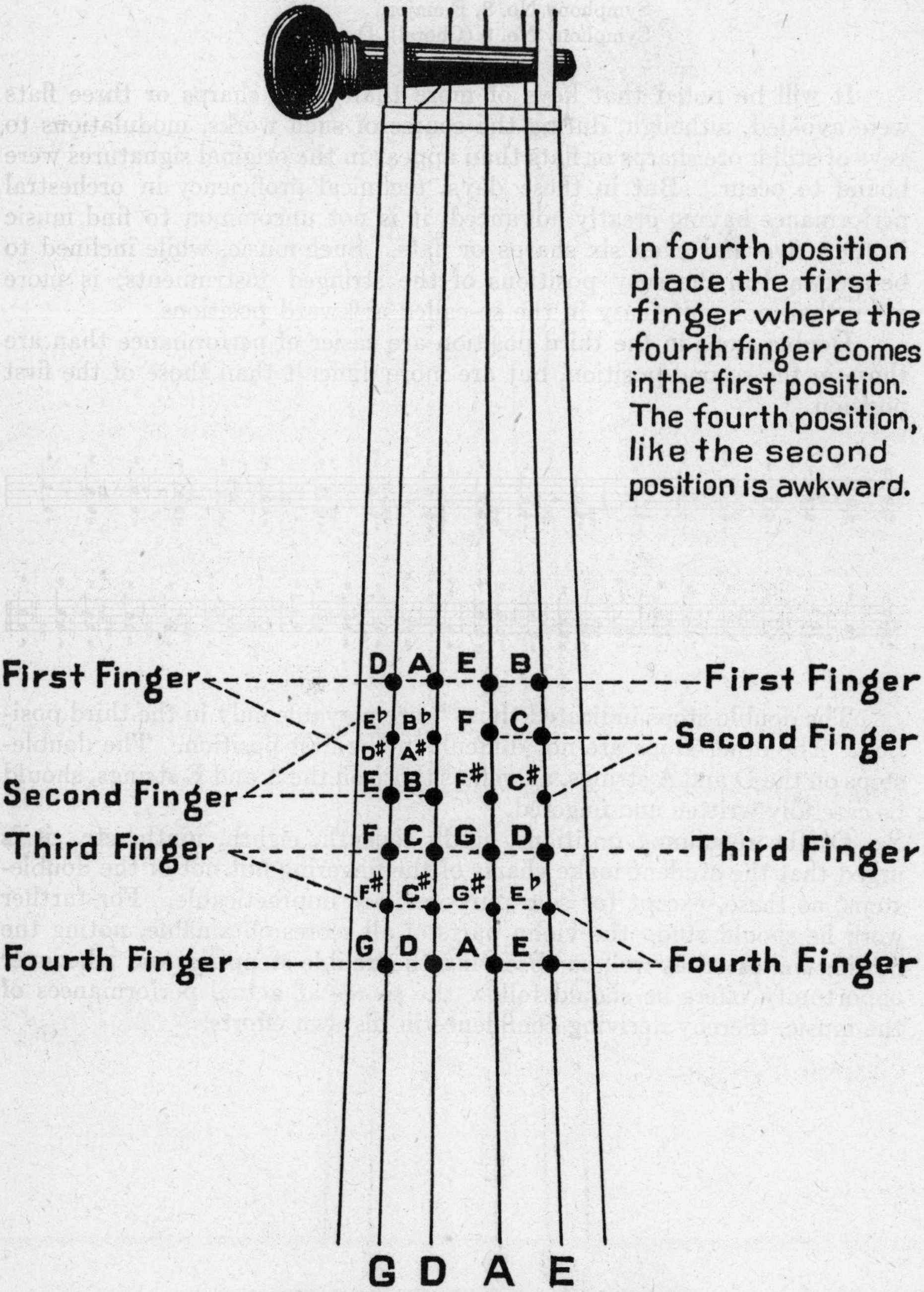

In fourth position place the first finger where the fourth finger comes in the first position. The fourth position, like the second position is awkward.

First Finger — — — D A E B — — — First Finger

E♭ B♭ F C — — Second Finger
D# A#

Second Finger — — — E B F# C#

Third Finger — — — F C G D — — — Third Finger

F# C# G# E♭

Fourth Finger — — — G D A E — — — Fourth Finger

G D A E
VIOLIN FINGER BOARD

The double stops should be carefully written and fingered in the fourth position, and those not found in other positions should be indicated and studied with a view to their future use in orchestration.

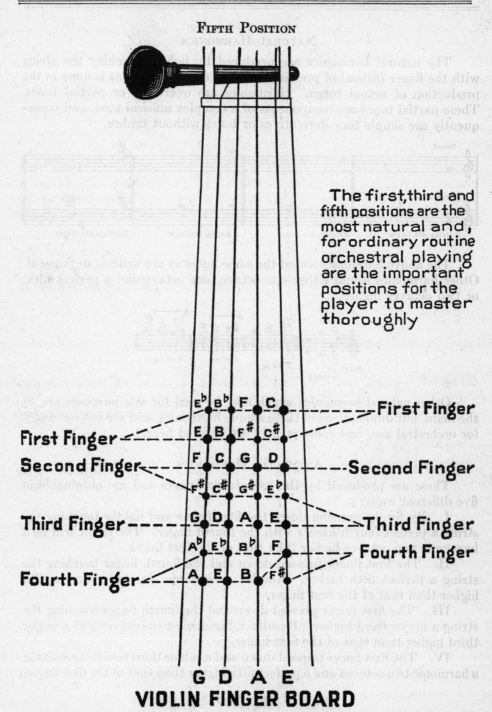

FIFTH POSITION

The first, third and fifth positions are the most natural and, for ordinary routine orchestral playing are the important positions for the player to master thoroughly

VIOLIN FINGER BOARD

The student should write all the double stops in the fifth position, fingering the same carefully and indicating those that are not found in other positions.

NATURAL HARMONICS

The natural harmonics are produced by lightly touching the string with the finger instead of pressing it firmly on the string, as is done in the production of actual tones. Harmonics are overtones or partial tones. These partial tones are components of a complex musical tone, and consequently are simple tone-derivatives or tones without timbre.

The above harmonics sound the same notes as are written, or fingered. Other harmonics sound either one octave, one octave and a perfect fifth, or two octaves higher.

Other natural harmonics which may be used for solo purposes are, in the main, but duplications of these simple harmonics, and are not necessary for orchestral use, and consequently are omitted here.

ARTIFICIAL HARMONICS

These are produced by the use of two fingers and are obtainable in five different ways:

I. By firmly pressing down the first finger and lightly touching the string a perfect fourth higher with the fourth finger. The result will be a harmonic two octaves higher than that of the first finger.

II. The first finger pressed down and the fourth finger touching the string a perfect fifth higher. Result: a harmonic an octave and a fifth higher than that of the first finger.

III. The first finger pressed down and the fourth finger touching the string a major third higher. Result: a harmonic two octaves and a major third higher than that of the first finger.

IV. The first finger pressed down and a minor third touched results in a harmonic two octaves and a perfect fifth higher than that of the first finger.

V. The most difficult method of all is the pressure of the first finger with the fourth finger touching the string an octave higher. The result will be a harmonic an octave above the first finger. This method is rarely used, as very few violinists are endowed with the stretch of an octave.

Of these five methods of production the first is the most commonly used for orchestral purposes. The method of notation is as follows:

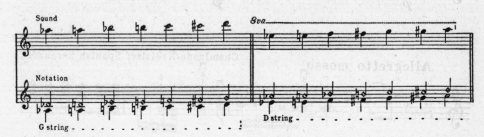

The student should complete the harmonics on the A and E strings in the above manner.

In scoring harmonics for orchestra the tones that are actually to be heard should be indicated in the music, as this facilitates the interpretation of the composition on the part of the conductor.

These harmonics offer no difficulties to the experienced orchestral player if played in slow tempo, but are difficult of performance in rapid tempo.

Mendelssohn's *Songs Without Words*

Exercise I.   Arrange the introduction, treble clef, of No. 28, for two violins, using double-stops for one or the other of the two instruments. Indicate fingering.

Exercise II.   Transpose the first eight measures of No. 2 an octave higher and arrange for three violins.   Finger.

Exercise III.   Finger the last seven measures of No. 5.

Exercise IV.   Transpose the first four measures of No. 20 an octave higher and notate for artificial harmonics.

Exercise V.   Write a short composition of eight or sixteen measures for two violins incorporating double-stops in the first position for the second violin while the first violin carries the melody in the first and third positions.

EXAMPLES OF NATURAL AND ARTIFICIAL HARMONICS

Albert E. Wier: "Danse Tzigane"

Chaminade-Kreisler: "Spanish Serenade"

Ernest Walker: "String Quartet in D"

Albert Spalding: "Etchings"

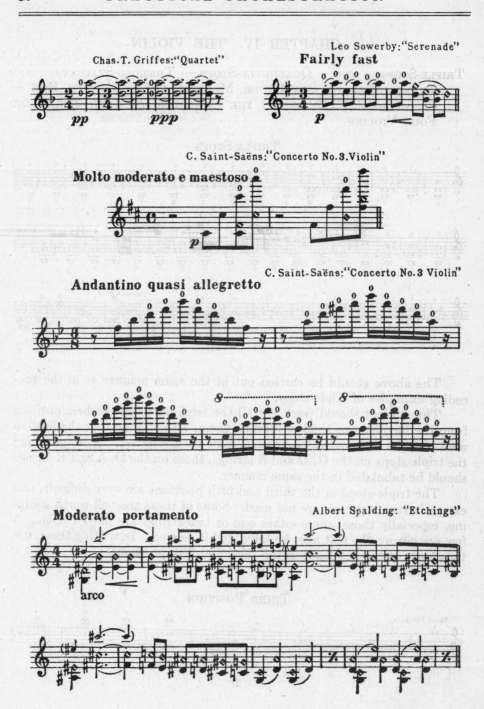

CHAPTER IV. THE VIOLIN

Triple-Stops and Quadruple-Stops — Tremolo-Staccato and Tremolo-Legato and Other Manners of Using the Bow — Examples — Exercises in the Combining of Two, Three and Four Violins

TRIPLE-STOPS

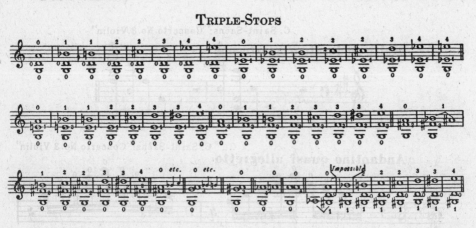

The above should be carried out in the same manner as in the preceding examples of triple-stops.

The student should work out all the triple-stops in the first position from the foregoing method of forming them. He will see that the bottom note changes chromatically upward with each new set. After finishing the triple-stops on the G, D and A strings, those on the D, A and E strings should be tabulated in the same manner.

The triple-stops in the third and fifth positions are very difficult, and except in rare instances are not used. Some of these are well worth studying, especially those where either one or two strings are played open. A few are given; the rest may be tabulated if desired. In writing these, use the charts of the keyboard in the third and fifth positions.

THIRD POSITION

QUADRUPLE-STOPS

Chords of four notes are also playable, and are very often used in cadences. Those which are necessary in orchestral playing are herewith given, and others may be tabulated from the charts of the violin finger board in third and fifth positions.

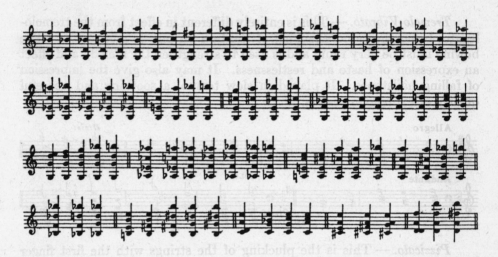

These quadruple-stops are also playable in arpeggio form as well as in a variety of ornamental figures.

OTHER VARIETIES OF BOWINGS

Tremolo-Legato. — This is a rapid, undulating repetition of two notes on the same string; consequently only intervals of seconds, thirds, fourths and possibly fifths can be used. The holding down of one finger on the string likens the effect to a trill.

This form of bowing is often utilized in rustling effects, and is frequently divided between the violins in order to gain in effect and smoothness.

Tremolo-Vibrato. — This is entirely different in effect from the tremolo-legato, being the rapid changing of the bow on one or more notes. The bowing must be very rapid and is used to strengthen the melody and effect an expression of haste and restlessness. It may also give the impression of falling hailstones. If played in slow tempo, a soothing and peaceful quality of expression results.

Pizzicato. — This is the plucking of the strings with the first finger of the bowing hand while retaining the bow in the same hand in order to change immediately to bowed tones. The pizzicato is very effective for certain compositions, such as serenades, light, airy dances, etc. It is not only used for melodies, but also for double-stops, triple-stops and quadruple-stops, the last especially in cadences. Pizzicato accompaniments to melodies or solos are frequently employed, and give a bright, crisp, cheerful color when carefully and properly used. It is indicated "pizz." The change to bowed tones is marked "arco." Discretion should be used in providing time to make the change.

Violin Mute. — When it is desirable to soften or veil the tone-color of the violin, a mute made of wood or metal is affixed to the bridge, thus reducing the tone to a minimum. This is useful in both the tremolo-vibrato and legato passages when a certain soft, ethereal color is desired. It is also useful in mysterious effects, particularly where the composer is depicting "atmosphere." It is indicated "with mute" or "con sordino." The release of the mute should be plainly indicated: "without mute" or "senza sordino."

Playing with the Back of the Bow. — In rare instances a brittle, almost empty tonal color is desired from the stringed instruments. This is obtained by striking the strings with the back, or wooden stick, of the bow. It is indicated "col legno" or "with back of bow." The change back to the hair side of the bow should be plainly marked "arco."

It is through the medium of the bow that the player expresses the art of the composer. It is, therefore, quite evident that the composer must give full directions as to how the music is to be bowed if he expects the performer to carry out his ideas and feelings. A succession of notes intended to be performed legato should be properly slurred into groups for this effect, as otherwise, if played with single strokes of the bow, the effect intended would be completely lost. The correct and detailed bowing of the stringed instruments in orchestrating serves to bring the characteristic and descriptive power of the music more and more into the foreground. It is, then, only natural that the student of orchestration should make a thorough study of the technic of the bow in order that there will be no doubt in the mind of the player as to what the proper bow procedure should be.

Mendelssohn's *Songs Without Words*

Exercise I. Beginning with the last chord in the second measure of No. 16, arrange the following nine measures for two violins, using double-stops and triple-stops garnered from the chord formations and rearranged to suit the purpose desired. The melody must be kept intact.

Exercise II. Arrange the first eight measures of No. 23 for three violins, transposing the final figure in the last measure one octave higher.

Exercise III. Arrange the first eight measures of No. 38 for three violins, transposing to a suitable key and shifting the low bass notes an octave higher to suit the violin range.

Exercise IV. Beethoven *Sonata*, Op. 10, No. 1. Arrange the first eighteen measures for two violins, double-stopping the principal chords in both instruments and carrying the theme in the first violin.

Exercise V. Compose eight or sixteen measures for a quartet of violins, employing double-stops, triple-stops and quadruple-stops in first position.

EXAMPLES OF TRIPLE-STOPS AND QUADRUPLE-STOPS AND TECHNICAL PASSAGES IN THE VARIOUS POSITIONS

Cecil Burleigh: "Violin Concerto in E minor"

Slowly

Allegretto moderato

Delibes: "Sylvia"

Presto

6th Position   3d Position   1st Position

Moderato

Albert Spaulding:"Alabama"

Double trill. Difficult.

Slowly

1st position

Open sustained note under chromatics. Not difficult.

Moderato

pizz.

Left hand pizzicato in combination with arco.

Presto

Very difficult, especially in fast tempo.

Albert Spalding: "Etchings"

C. Saint-Saëns:"Concerto No. 3 Violin"

Molto moderato e maestoso

Allegro non troppo

Allegro

Difficult position shifts.

Sostenuto   Rachmaninoff-Elman:"Serenade"

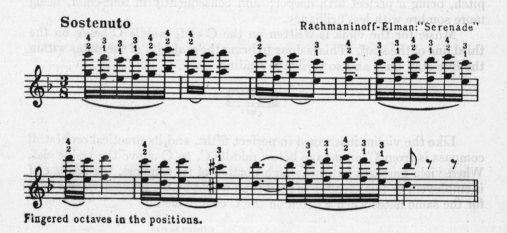

Fingered octaves in the positions.

Andantino   Pablo Sarasate:"Spanish Dance"

Left hand pizzacato. (+ Plucked)

Struck with
the ivory tip
of the bow.   Leo Sowerby:"String Quartet in G Major"

Fairly fast

CHAPTER V. THE VIOLA

Italian: *Viola*
French: *Alto*
German: *Bratsche*

FINGERING OF FIRST AND THIRD POSITIONS — DIAGRAM OF FINGER
BOARD — DOUBLE-STOPS IN BOTH POSITIONS — BOWING — EX-
AMPLES — EXERCISES IN COMBINATION WITH VIOLINS

The viola differs from the violin in size, being somewhat larger; in
pitch, being a perfect fifth deeper; and consequently in tone-color, being
more sombre with less brilliancy.

Music for the viola is written on the C clef, middle C being on the
third line of the staff. This is done to bring the majority of the notes within
the five staff lines and so facilitate reading.

Like the violin, it is tuned in perfect fifths, and its practical orchestral
compass is from C, an octave below middle C, to C above the treble clef.
When viola passages lie in the high portion of its compass, the treble clef
is employed, as this is easier to read than would be the necessary leger lines
for the same notes when written on the C or alto clef.

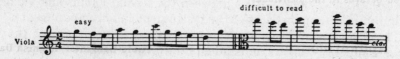

The three upper strings of the viola are the same as the three lower
strings of the violin. The lowest, or C, string is metal-wound and is dark,
hard and dull in character. The quality of the G string is strikingly lovely
and almost human in sound. The D string is also attractive in quality,
and the A string has a mellow, though somewhat strident, tone-color
especially in its upper register.

The viola is the alto voice of the string section of the orchestra, and
does a great deal of the filling in of the harmonies employed under the melody
of the first violins. Its sombreness does not make of it an assertive instrument, and at times its rhythm alone is more noticeable than its tone emis-
sion. Double-stops and short counter-melodies seem to be its chief mission
in the ensemble of the orchestra, although it is occasionally given a short

solo passage to perform. However, there is a tendency among modern composers to emphasize the importance of the viola as a solo instrument.

The fingering of the viola is similar to that of the violin, but being a larger instrument the tones necessitate larger stretches of the fingers between the notes.

The principal positions, as on the violin, are the first, third and fifth, although the second and fourth positions should be carefully studied and tabulated for the sake of thoroughness in technical proficiency in scoring.

A great many examples of viola writing could be quoted for study by the student, but a few are herewith tabulated for certain desirable and effective uses of the instrument in conjunction with other orchestral voices.

Beethoven's C minor *Symphony*, adagio movement, illustrates the reinforcement of the cello melody by the violas, adding roundness and purity to the tone.

Mozart's *Trio*, for clarinet, viola and piano, offers splendid illustrations of the viola's general technical uses.

Brahm's *Sextet* in B♭ major, and *Quintet* in G major, Op. 111, contain so many masterly uses of the viola in such a variety of technical display as to offer an almost complete study of the instrument.

The string trios and quartets of Mozart and Beethoven will all bear careful investigation as to the uses of the viola, and a great deal can be gleaned from such study, especially in the way of doublings in the melody with the lower tones of the violins or the upper tones of the cellos, the interlocking of double stops between the second violins and violas, and the rhythmic arpeggio effects of the instrument in accompaniments.

There have not been many solos or concerti written for the viola, although all viola players, as students, have familiarized themselves with David's *Concertino*, Op. 12, Schumann's *Four Pieces*, Op. 113, Joachim's *Hebrew Melodies*, Op. 10, Kalliwoda's *Six Nocturnes*, Op. 186, and Wallner's *Fantasie de Concert*.

York Bowen has written two very effective sonatas for viola and piano.

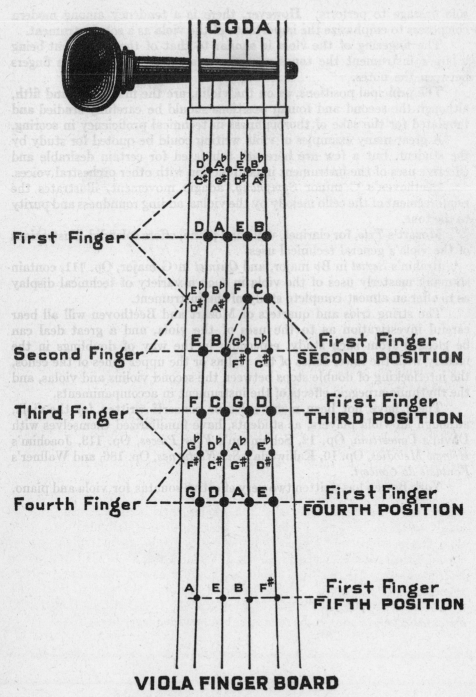

VIOLA FINGER BOARD

Charts of the second, third, fourth and fifth positions should be made.

DOUBLE-STOPS FOR THE VIOLA

Tables of the double-stops on the G and D strings as well as on the D and A strings should be written and carefully fingered.

BOWING

The bowing of the viola is in every way similar to that of the violin. Care should be taken always to see that the first and second violins and violas are bowing as nearly as possible in unison. This will not be difficult if it is always kept in mind that the strong accent of the measure should have the down bow except in involved and intricate passages where it is necessary to use a variety of bowings on the various stringed instruments.

The tremolo-legato and tremolo-staccato bowings may be used in conjunction with the same bowings as on the violins; but as the viola section is rarely so divided, this is never effective unless the violins are assisting.

In many concerti for strings, which at present appear to be much in vogue, some sections, especially the violins, are often divided into as many as three or four parts. The violas are rarely divided into more than two sections, and, when it is necessary to do so, individual staves should be used and indicated, — Viola I, Viola II and Viola III. Whenever instruments are "divisi," use a separate staff for each division and bracket them together in groups. If, in the divided violas, the part to be played by Viola I lies well in the upper register, use the G clef rather than the C clef, as this will eliminate the use of the many added leger lines.

A Variety of Viola Technic

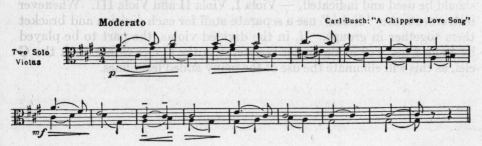

Mendelssohn's *Songs Without Words*

Exercise I. Transpose No. 14 to E minor and arrange the first eight measures for three violins and one viola.

Exercise II. Arrange and finger the first eight measures of the Rondo, Beethoven *Sonata*, Op. 13, for one violin and one viola.

Exercise III. Arrange and finger the first sixteen measures of the Allegretto, Beethoven *Sonata*, Op. 27, No. 2, for three violins and one viola.

Exercise IV. Compose a short piece for three violins and one viola.

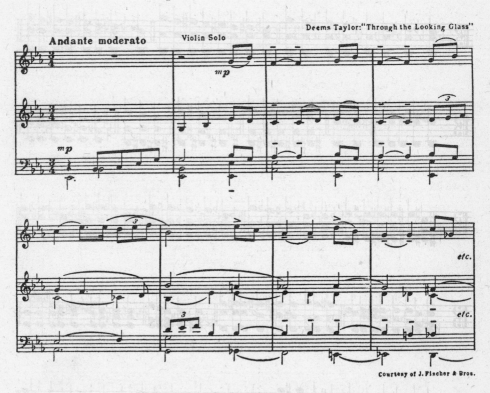

Deems Taylor: "Through the Looking Glass"

Courtesy of J. Fischer & Bros.

This excerpt is taken from the original sketch of *Through the Looking Glass*, and serves to illustrate how the composer jots down his ideas preparatory to setting them into the orchestral frame.

CHAPTER VI. THE VIOLA

REMAINING POSITIONS — TRIPLE-STOPS AND QUADRUPLE-STOPS — NATURAL AND ARTIFICIAL HARMONICS — CHARACTER OF TONE-COLOR IN CONJUNCTION WITH VIOLINS — EXERCISES

TRIPLE-STOPS

The triple-stops on the G, D and A strings should be tabulated in the same manner as those on the C, G and D strings. These triple-stops are all in the first position and are not difficult to perform, as all the awkward stops have been omitted.

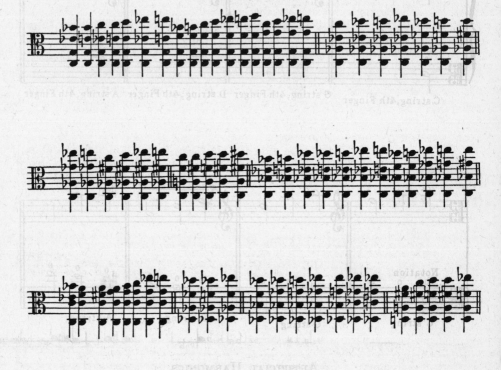

QUADRUPLE-STOPS

NATURAL HARMONICS

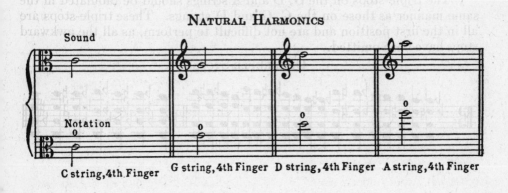

ARTIFICIAL HARMONICS

Of the various methods of producing artificial harmonics, those used for the violin are again applicable to the viola.

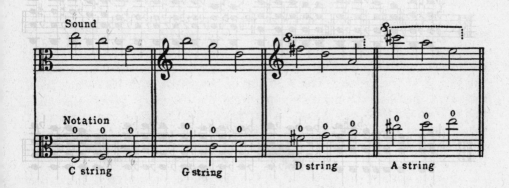

The harmonics on the D and A strings should be written carefully in the manner shown above.

The first and third positions are those mostly employed in ordinary orchestral routine, but the average player should have the seven positions at his command. He will find very little need for the artificial harmonics herein presented, but the thorough student of orchestration should know these, as the music of the present embodies effects formed from these in combination with the harmonics of the other strings.

TONE-COLOR

The color of the viola when used with other strings is barren of prominence. It fills in comfortably, but does not add brilliance or decisiveness to the ensemble. It does, however, give depth and warmth to the general effect, and adds the charm of the alto voice so necessary in filling the gap between the violin and the cello sections. The dark color of the lower strings is used for characteristic purposes and expressions, such as awe, sorrow, pain, troubles of a humorous nature and kindred imaginings. The upper strings are more assertive but not aggressively so, as they are easily overshadowed by the higher vibrations of violins and somewhat subdued by the power of the cellos. The A string of the viola, with its rather nasal quality, is perhaps the most effective from the viewpoint of assertiveness, and this should be borne in mind when it is desired to make the instrument speak against the brother strings. The other strings should then be somewhat tempered to the effect desired of the viola, and not allowed to overbalance it.

But, as has already been stated, the viola is very essential in the make-up of the string color in the orchestra as well as in the string quartet. In the latter, the duties of the viola become more individualized. Its prominence in the theme-carrying is more assertive, as it has less competition from instruments which tend to lessen its carrying power through the absorption of its overtones. The tender warmth of its color is more defined, and consequently the instrument becomes more elemental in purpose in the quartet setting.

In the orchestra, the viola is seen but rarely heard to any great extent unless it is performing in a solo passage or over very subdued accompaniment. Its main uses appear to be those of harmonic fillings by means of double-stops or added melodies and rhythmic stimulation, all of which adds greatly to the tonal warmth and depth of orchestral expression.

Examples of Viola Technic: Stops, Bowings, Harmonics

Mendelssohn's *Songs Without Words*

Exercise I. Arrange the first sixteen measures of No. 20 for solo violin with accompaniment of two violins and one viola. Transpose to F major and omit the lower notes of the bass in measures 1, 2, 3, 10 and 11.

Exercise II. Transcribe a suitable song or hymn for violins and viola.

Exercise III. Compose a viola solo in the following manner:

VIOLA D'AMORE

French: *Viola d'Amour*
German: *Liebergeige*

The viola d'amore is slightly larger in size than the viola, which instrument it preceded. It is at present rarely used, not alone because of its antiquity, but because of its limitations. The instrument boasts of fourteen strings, seven of which are actually employed in performance, and seven wire strings which are placed below the bridge and under the finger board and which act as sympathetic vibrators. The upper or playable strings, which are of catgut (the three lowest being wire-wound), are tuned in thirds and fourths according to the D major triad:

The music for the viola d'amore may be written on the alto C clef or the treble G clef, usually the latter, in spite of the necessary added leger lines. The range of the instrument is about three octaves and a fifth, all of which is playable in the various color gradations. Since the instrument is tuned in D major, many difficulties arise when it is played in other than nearly related keys. In flat keys the sympathetic strings are either silent or sympathetic only occasionally when the harmonies permit. Some of the best keys for which to score the instrument are D, A and G major, B, F♯ and E minor.

One of the great difficulties in connection with the use of the instrument is keeping it in tune. The seven sympathetic strings must always be strictly in tune with the playable strings, and this keeps the performer constantly occupied and worried.

The tone-color of the viola d'amore is somewhat similar to that of the viola, though more mysterious and *spirituelle* in atmosphere, due to the sympathetic vibrations of the under strings. Arpeggios and large chords are easily performed in almost any variety of tempo, and a peculiar loveliness of effect results in melody passages.

Harmonics on the instrument are easily obtainable in the usual variety

of methods:

As there are various methods of obtaining one and the same tone in harmonics, the performer may find that the task of deciphering the riddle of just which method to use is left to his judgment, the score reading as

follows:

This is rather unfair to the performer who has to keep fourteen unruly strings in perfect tune, and the student is urged to use the first method of notation.

The viola d'amore has been employed by Meyerbeer, Bach and other masters, both as an obbligato voice and as an orchestral voice. In the latter capacity it has never been employed to more telling advantage than in *La Mort de Tintagiles,* by Ch. M. Loeffler, a short excerpt of which follows:

Ch. M. Loeffler: "La Mort de Tintagiles"

Violoncello

CHAPTER VII. THE VIOLONCELLO

Italian: *Violoncello*
French: *Violoncelle*
German: *Violoncell*

First Position — Diagram showing Fingering — Double-Stops — Bowing — Examples — Exercises in Combination with Violins and Viola

The violoncello, or cello, as it is commonly called, is the tenor or baritone voice of the string section of the orchestra. The instrument is four-stringed, and is pitched one octave deeper than the viola. Like the violin and viola it is tuned in fifths, the two lower strings being metal-wound like

those of the viola.

Notation for the cello is on the bass clef, but, if necessary, the tenor and occasionally the violin, or G, clef may be used in order to avoid the necessity of reading leger lines over the bass clef.

The range for orchestral purposes is from low C to C on the G clef, although Strauss and other modern composers occasionally exceed this limit.

Orchestral Range.   Solo Range.

There are seven available positions, it being necessary in the top positions to use the thumb sidewise across the strings in order to stop the vibrations at certain points, thus allowing freedom of action for the four fingers in the production of the high tones. It will rarely be necessary for the orchestral writer to use these high positions, and the fingering of the same should be left entirely to the discretion of the player.

The cello is a much larger instrument than the viola, and is bowed from the side carrying the lowest string. The player holds the cello between his knees and secures it firmly to the floor by means of a pointed metal extension through the button. While the instrument seems rather

55

cumbersome and unwieldy in shape and size, it is, nevertheless, easily and gracefully handled, and all seeming obstacles are readily overcome or minimized by the performer.   There are certain things on every instrument that require thought and reflection before adoption because of ungainliness in technic and consequently in effect produced.   Skips of fourths are especially to be avoided on the cello, whereas these are not at all difficult on the violin or viola.   This is due chiefly to the fingering, which is quite different on the cello.   This does not mean that every interval of a fourth should be avoided in writing for the instrument, but that figures involving repetitions of fourths in passage work are difficult owing to the fingering. Fourths can be negotiated with ease in a straight melody in either fast or slow tempo, provided there is not a series of them with which to contend.

The following diagram of the cello finger board is not reproduced in its actual size, as was done with both the violin and viola, as space will not permit of this:

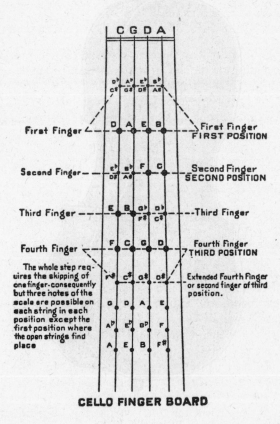

CELLO FINGER BOARD

Violoncello, Back

DOUBLE-STOPS

Double-stopping on the cello is less frequent in orchestral playing than in solo playing, and consequently but few double-stops are necessary to learn. The student may tabulate more double-stops than are indicated in the illustrations given below. All double-stops wherein one string is open are not difficult of performance, but those involving two fingers are not only awkward in fast passages but also unsatisfactory.

The bowing of the cello is similar to that of the violin and viola, except that the instrument is exactly opposite in the arrangement of its strings. The higher strings are to the left, whereas on the violin the highest string is to the right. This results from the cello being played in front of the performer instead of being held between the chin and left shoulder. The various technical bowings, such as legato, staccato, etc., are all playable, and are indicated in the same manner as for the violin and viola.

The song of the cello is very effective, especially when other instruments of the orchestra are subordinated to its melodic utterance. It speaks in its gracious, appealing tenor quality, at once romantic, forceful and dignified. It carries the theme in a sure, sweeping manner, and counter-melodizes in a distinctive, grateful and satisfactory style.

In conjunction with other instruments it is equally gratifying in its duties of doublings, reinforcings, harmonic fillings, rhythmic accentuations and the sustaining of pedal points and figures. Altogether the cello should command the respect and admiration of the composer to the point where he will feel it his duty to study the technical possibilities of the instrument in every detail.

EXAMPLES ILLUSTRATING CELLO TECHNIC

EXERCISES IN COMBINATION WITH VIOLINS AND VIOLA

EXERCISES IN COMBINATION WITH VIOLINS AND VIOLA

EXERCISES IN COMBINATION WITH VIOLINS AND VIOLA

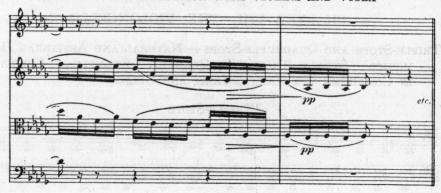

Mendelssohn's *Songs Without Words*

Exercise I. Arrange eleven measures of No. 9 for string quartet.

Exercise II. Arrange sixteen measures of No. 25 for violin, viola and cello.

Exercise III. Arrange a baritone song for a solo cello and string quartet.

Exercise IV. Arrange the first sixteen measures of the second movement of the Beethoven *Sonata*, Op. 10, No. 1, for string quartet.

Exercise V. Compose a short string quartet in the large primary form.

CHAPTER VIII. THE VIOLONCELLO

TRIPLE-STOPS AND QUADRUPLE-STOPS — NATURAL AND ARTIFICIAL HARMONICS — STRING TRIO AND QUARTET — EXAMPLES — EXERCISES IN COMBINING THE VIOLIN, VIOLA AND CELLO

TRIPLE-STOPS

The triple-stops indicated in the above illustration are all easily playable; and while the list is far from complete, these are possibly the most commonly used. As on the violin and viola, these may be played as broken chords or arpeggios, or as tone figures with a variety of different bowings.

The quadruple-stops for the cello, while effective in solo passages, do not so frequently occur in orchestral music. However, they are worthy of the student's careful and discriminating consideration, and may find greater opportunity in modern music than in the music of the older school.

The foregoing quadruple-stops are all playable, mostly in the first position. Other quadruple-stops may be formulated by using the finger board on page 56.

THE NATURAL HARMONICS

THE ARTIFICIAL HARMONICS

These are produced with thumb position and fourth finger lightly touching the string a perfect fourth higher.

The artificial harmonics on the D and A strings should be carefully worked out in the manner indicated above.

EXAMPLES OF CELLO TECHNIC

Mendelssohn's *Songs Without Words*

Exercise I. Arrange the first sixteen measures of No. 25 for string quartet.

Exercise II. Arrange the first fifteen measures of No. 30 for string quartet. Pizzicato accompaniment.

Exercise III. Transpose to the key of G major and arrange the first sixteen measures of No. 33 for string quartet.

Exercise IV. Arrange the first sixteen measures of *Sonata* No. 3, Op. 2, No. 3, Beethoven, for string quartet.

Exercise V. Compose a "Melody" for cello with string accompaniment in the large three-part primary form.

Exercise VI. Write the first movement of a sonatina for cello with piano accompaniment; using occasional double-stops and natural harmonics for the solo instrument.

CHAPTER IX. THE DOUBLE–BASS (CONTRABASS)

Italian: *Contrabasso*
French: *Contre basse*
German: *Kontra bass*

FINGERING, BOWING AND HARMONICS — EXAMPLES — EXERCISES

The double-bass, the largest of the stringed instruments, is a most important member of the orchestra. Its solidness in rhythm, its strength in upholding the harmonic mass, and its bigness in the sustaining of rich tonal effects make of it an indispensable factor to be carefully studied for balance and body.

We have two varieties with which to deal: the four-stringed and the five-stringed instruments. The former is the more commonly employed, although the five-stringed bass finds place in many of our large symphony orchestras.

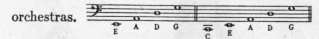

There still exists a three-stringed double-bass which is tuned in fourths or fifths but which is not used in this country.

It is often found on the European Continent, especially in the smaller cities and villages of France and Germany, where it is used in the small theatre or dance orchestras.

The double-bass is the only stringed instrument for which, in writing, we have to consider transposition. It sounds a full octave lower than the written note, and consequently all parts must be written an octave higher than they are expected to sound.

The range is from first E, below the bass clef, to the second B♭ above the bass clef. Considering the transposition, the actual range in sound is:

Sound

Written

66

The Double Bass or Contrabass

The five-stringed double-bass has a third added below this range, but this is rarely used, as the difficulty in producing these tones on the fifth string, especially in fast passages, is very great.

The performer on the bass has far more difficulties to overcome than has any other stringed-instrument performer. The awkwardness of the handling of so large an instrument is in itself a big problem. The player usually stands or leans against a high stool. A bow of heavy proportions is used. The heavy, slowly vibrating strings require great finger strength in stopping, and in the higher positions two fingers must be used for this purpose, while the other fingers support them in holding down the string.

The first, second and fourth fingers are used up to the sixth position, the third finger always supporting the fourth in stopping the string. In the sixth position the third finger is used because the fourth is not long enough for the stretches required, as it circles away from the point where stopping is required.

In fingering the double-bass, support to the stoppings should always be given by the unused fingers behind that actually stopping a tone. For instance, if the second finger is being utilized, the first finger should also be pressing the string directly behind it; if the third finger is being used, the first and second fingers should be pressing down the string at the same time; if the fourth finger is in use, all three remaining fingers should be supporting the fourth.

There are two methods in common use, but the method of fingering described above is that generally adopted.

Chromatic and diatonic scale passages, all varieties of melodies, and even arpeggios are playable on the double-bass, although many of these technical requirements sound clearer and become easier of performance if doubled with the cello or another low-pitched instrument of the orchestra.

In dance music the marking (one might almost say pounding) of the double-basses on the strong accent of each measure is a well-recognized characteristic feature. The instrument performs a like service in a lesser, though just as important, degree in all compositions in which the strings are employed. It is less frequently used for obbligato or solo passages than the other strings, but could be so employed to excellent effect were the capabilities of the instrument better understood by orchestral composers.

BOWINGS

The bowing, so far as indications and markings are concerned, is virtually the same as for the other strings. With the exception of the spiccato bowing, and due consideration for the number of notes possible for each stroke (these being considerably fewer because of the strength required), there is very little to mention. Figures in which wide skips are to be performed are rather difficult unless between neighboring strings, one of which is open.

When one or two strings have to be crossed by the bow in making wide skips, the effect is very unsatisfactory and should be avoided, except, possibly, in very slow tempi.

Simplification is often necessary in parts where rapid passage work is required. This is easily accomplished if the cello or bassoon is assisting.

The cello and double-bass often double in playing the bass line in simple compositions, the two instruments sounding an octave apart; but wherever involved contrapuntal figuration occurs, the simplification of the bass part is advisable, and will add greatly to the strength of the desired effect.

Quick passages at the bottom of the bass range are most unsatisfactory unless the staccato bowing (one note to each bow) is used, which somewhat clarifies the intention; but slurred passages such as the following are not only ineffective but barely audible, especially in tutti.

The foregoing passage would be still more effective if simplification were resorted to, the cellos taking the contrapuntal line and the basses the skeleton of the figure.

NATURAL HARMONICS

Only the natural harmonics are employed for the double-bass, as the artificial harmonics are too difficult and uncertain of performance. Those indicated are commonly employed but rarely used for orchestral purposes.

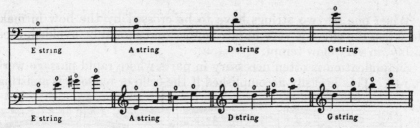

The harmonics shown above on the second staff are possible of performance in several ways, particularly those on the D string; but the player will use his own judgment in their performance, and only those indicated by the "o" over them need be written, as all others are quite impossible of performance.

The lower strings of the double-bass are dark in color, suggestive of tragedy and mystery in certain phases, and of sorrow and lament in others. The upper strings are more bright and strident and useful for full string coloration. The lower strings, when used for single harmonic tones, give body to the chord formation above, and thus add strength to the ensemble. The upper two strings perform this same duty in a somewhat less effective manner. Tremolos are not successful on the double-bass because of the amount of energy required on the part of the performer. They should be given to the cello section of the orchestra while the double-bass plays notes of twice the time value as those being executed in tremolo by the cello and other strings.

The use of the pizzicato should be somewhat tempered for the double-bass, as in the upper positions it is rather unsatisfactory, and in very fast work in the lower positions it is hard to get a firm, clear tone because of the difficulty in stopping the strings quickly enough. Slow pizzicato is very effective and telling, especially with an occasional open string.

In the foregoing illustration it will be noted that the basses are divided, thus making the pizzicato easier of performance.

In the preceding example the first violins are doubling in unison with the clarinet in A which is playing the melody as a solo. Note the quiet, simple string accompaniment.

Illustrating triple and quadruple stops in the strings.

Mendelssohn's *Songs Without Words*

Exercise I. Arrange the last sixteen measures of No. 27 for string orchestra, using divided strings wherever necessary.

Exercise II. Make a free arrangement of the last eighteen measures of No. 40 for string orchestra.

Exercise III. Arrange the first twenty measures of the Allegro Vivace from *Sonata* No. 13, Op. 27, No. 1, Beethoven, for string orchestra.

Exercise IV. Write a waltz in regulation dance form, for string orchestra, employing pizzicato bass, at times, and double-stops in the second violins and violas.

Exercise V. Arrange a well-known song for voice and string orchestra.

Exercise VI. Compose a serenade for string orchestra in the scherzo form.

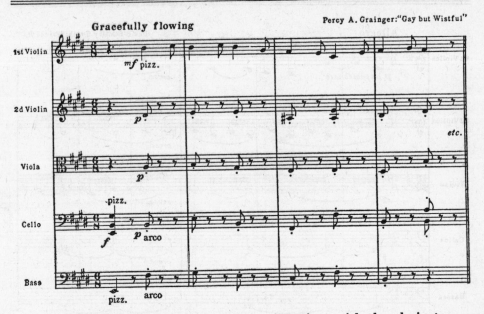

Above the first violins are doubling in unison with the clarinets.

An example of unison in the strings.

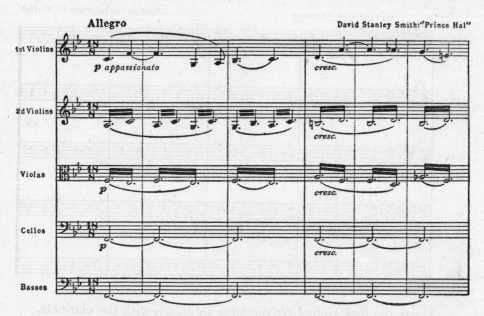

Tremolo accompaniment in second violins and violas.

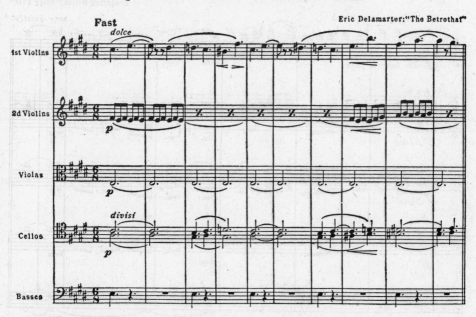

Cellos duetting over pedals in violas and basses; second violins performing a tremolo figure; melody in first violins.

Andante   Helen Dallam: Sea Pictures."A Calm Day"

An example of string orchestra, illustrating divided strings in sustained harmonies under the melody carried in the solo section of the divided first violins.

Example of the melody in tremolo — staccato in octaves in the violins.

Violin solo on the G string with soft accompaniment by the other string voices.

Eric Delamarter:"Overture. The Faun"

Tremolo staccato and divided strings.

Leo Sowerby:"Set of Four"

Melody carried in octaves in violins; cellos and basses in octaves.

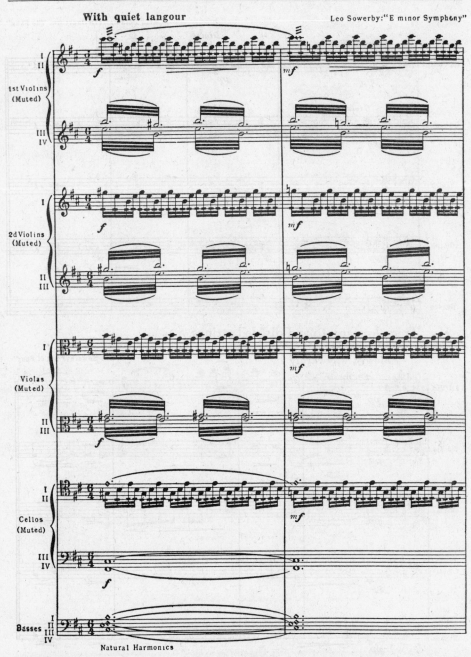

Example in divisi in which tremolo-legato and tremolo-staccato and natural harmonics are vividly illustrated. All muted except basses.

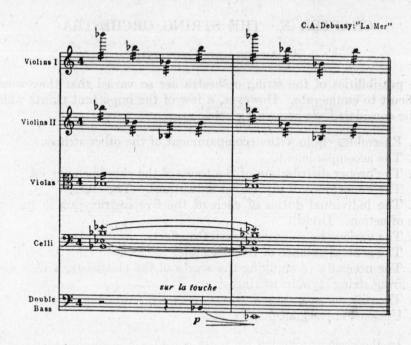

C.A. Debussy: "La Mer"

Allegro moderato

Antonio Vivaldi: "Concerto for Strings"
Arr by Sam Franko

CHAPTER X. THE STRING ORCHESTRA

Examples and Exercises

The possibilities of the string orchestra are so varied that they would be difficult to enumerate. However, a few of the important points which must be considered are herewith given.

1. Ensemble. Solo with accompaniment of the other strings.
2. The accompaniment.
3. The proper distribution of the tones of the chords employed.
4. The importance of expression indications. The mute.
5. The individual duties of each of the five instruments in its own sphere of action. Divisi.
6. The various bowings and pizzicato effects.
7. The general balance of the ensemble.
8. The necessity of studying the scores of the classicists, with a view to acquiring string style in writing.
9. The differences in tempi.
10. Unisons, entries, harmonics, etc.

1. In the string orchestra we must consider five singing voices with great ranges and all varieties of technic. Each factor in this orchestra is a potential solo instrument; any two instruments may sing a duet; any three, a trio; and in compositions involving contrapuntal voice leadings, such as fugues and quasi-fugues, all instruments may be of equal importance in the general ensemble.

If the first violins are to carry the solo melody, all other voices should be modified in tone-coloring by a shade so that the importance of the melody will be assertive rather than hidden. The difference should not be glaringly apparent. Occasionally the doubling of the melody in the octave adds definition and strength, and is of common occurrence, especially between the first violins and cellos.

2. The accompaniment, which may consist of double-stops in the second violins and violas, counter-melodies in the cellos, with the basses performing the underpinning chord-tones, should be carefully studied from the viewpoint of harmonic richness as well as of rhythmic variety. There are so many different forms of string accompaniment, from staccato counterpoint against the melody to pizzicato figuration, that it would be next to impossible to enumerate or classify them. The student should always study the scores of the well-known writers, observing especially those passages where the string section is carrying the burden of the composition.

3. The proper distribution of chord-tones has always been a problem. We have chosen always to double the root or fifth of major triads, and this is a good general rule to follow; but a great deal will depend upon the distribution of the chord-notes over the string range in determining how they should be managed.

When the chord is in its fundamental or root position, as follows;

we have very little to consider, for the doubling takes care of itself and is merely a question of double-stopping or triple-stopping or of divisi. But

when a simple four-note major triad is in question, such as,

and the distribution of notes must be made, it is always well to consider first of all the tone-color desired, which should help govern the doubling of the tones. In the first example (a) we find a chord arrangement that balances well and contains the root three times with no doubling of the third or fifth. In the distribution of the chord-notes at (b) the fifth is doubled to good effect. At (c) it was necessary to double the third in order to define the chord in its upper register. These three positions permit of any grade of tone-coloring from pp to fff, and may be employed in any variety of desired figuration. The third of a minor triad may be more freely doubled than the major third, as its disposition is never as assertive. When a major triad is in first inversion (third in the bass) and doubling is necessary, it should be done in unison or octave unless the chord is very full, in which case the third may occur in one of the upper voices, preferably in the alto.

In augmented and diminished triads the doubling has to be very carefully observed, as the assertiveness of the root of the diminished triad and the fifth of the augmented triad are so pronounced as to overbalance the rest of the chord if too freely doubled.

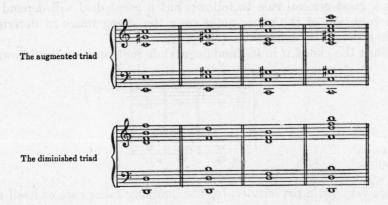

The augmented triad

The diminished triad

The doubling of the third of the dominant seventh chord in root position will depend upon the doubling of the other tones of the chord, as, for instance:

The dominant seventh
root position

If the dominant seventh is in first inversion, the third should be kept out of the upper voices of the chord, thus:

The dominant seventh
first inversion

In the second inversion of the dominant seventh chord the fifth may be doubled at will; but care should be shown in doubling the third, and unless the chord is eight-toned it should not contain more than one third.

In the third inversion the seventh of the chord should be kept out of the upper voices, and if doubled this should occur in the cello voice:

The dominant seventh
third inversion

The diminished seventh chord in root position is rarely written with the fundamental tone doubled except in the bass, and then only in an eight-note chord. In the first inversion the third should be kept out of the upper part of the chord unless the chord is very full. The second inversion, as well as the third inversion, should receive the same consideration.

The diminished seventh
in its various positions

4. The importance of impressing upon the student of orchestration the value of tonal indications cannot be too strongly urged. He should not be over-finicky in distributing his marks of expression, but he should be very considerate of the intention in mind, and make it forcefully clear so that the performer does not have to assert whatever powers of mind reading he may possess, and may give his undivided attention to the business at hand. In the use of the mutes, ample time must be allowed (at least a measure or two) for adjusting them as well as for their removal.

5. In considering the individual duties of the stringed instruments each should be taken into consideration. The first violins are the melody-carrying voices of the choir. They are expected to be technically proficient in the very high register. The second violins may occasionally take up the melody work, but are expected to fill in the harmonies or move in duet voicing with the first violins. The violas are the alto voices, sombre, refined, adding harmonies in the way of double-stops or counter-melodies. The cellos, the tenors of the string choir, are rich in melody-carrying power, especially when doubled in the lower octave with the first violins. They may also assist in the underpinning notes of the bass line by doubling an

octave higher with the double-basses, or they may, on occasion, carry the bass line where the deeper tones of the double-bass are not required. The double-basses are not alone the harmonic underpinning, but very strong factors in steadying the rhythmic ensemble. They do duty, also, in certain low-pitched ornamentation, including scale passages and arpeggios, tremolos and pedal-point.

When thickened voicing demands, each group of strings may be divided into two or three separate voices, thus adding fullness and richness to the general ensemble. The first violins are very often divided, the concert-master group assuming the upper voice, and the second concert-master group the lower voice. Each section may be divided in this manner.

6. A thorough knowledge of the various bowings will give a wonderful variety of effects to the strings, and should be carefully indicated in the scoring. The student should realize that uniformity of bowing is very important, and that he should arrange for this in his scoring. It is not necessary that all the bows should be moving up or down simultaneously all the time, but a general semblance of co-ordination should exist. The importance of bowing may be likened to the importance of phrasing, being so closely related as to be almost one. The plucked string, or pizzicato, adds rhythmic definition and variety of effect in compositions demanding lightness and deftness in interpretation. Pizzicato chords in the cadences are often very telling, particularly in *p* or *pp*.

7. It is not necessary that all the strings should be singing all of the time, as this would be entirely out of balance in the sense that monotony would result. Each group of the choir should have its regular duties to perform as well as its individual song to project, and its quiet, unassertive moments. Through a careful consideration of these facts a climax will be more insistent and of vitally greater import if approached in gradation of added voices rather than through added volume of strength in all the voices.

8. Through a careful study of the string sections of the chamber music and orchestral scores of such writers as Beethoven and other classicists, the student will derive an education in writing for strings that will give him great confidence and will propel his own endeavors. He should delve into these works with a view to learning a great many things that cannot be set down in print except through a very detailed description of each individual point.

He will very quickly discover that these writers had a thorough knowledge of each instrument for which they wrote, exhibiting a complete technical understanding of all the details characteristic of the medium employed. These standards of thoroughness are the foundation on which the student of orchestration should build. There should be nothing slipshod or haphazard in his writing. There should be no shirking of detail. In other words, if he is writing for the violin, it should be violin music that the performer will appreciate and enjoy playing. In doing this he will reap benefits in the way of a more sensitive interpretation of his work than would result if he left a great many things to the judgment of the performer. Instrumentalists are not mind readers, although they are often called upon to exhibit occult powers; and, in consequence, the more regard and respect the composer has for the performer, the greater will be his reward in thought and attention to detail.

9. A composition may be ruined through a lack of attention to tempi indications. Do not write a word of explanation at the beginning of a work, such as "allegro" or "fast," and expect it to be a "cut and dried" affair in which the conductor will recognize just where a rallentando or an accelerando should occur. Use plenty of tempi indications throughout, and remember that cadences require special attention. Cadences are the marks of punctuation in music, and should be regarded in the light of approaches of repose. They need not slow down unnecessarily, but should be a trifle more defined in tempi in order to delineate their significance.

10. The entire string body may be called upon to carry a melody in unison. This really means that the instruments are playing the same melody in their own registers, which may be an octave above or below that of another instrument, or, in some instances, two octaves higher or lower. This is called unison.[1] Very often the cellos and first violins will carry a melody in so-called unison. This doubling of the melody by another string voice is very effective at times, particularly in a tutti where strengthening becomes necessary.[2] The entrances of the string voices are sometimes arranged in a fugal manner, each instrument, from the lowest to the highest, or *vice versa*, entering in turn. This is a very characteristic opening and results in an interesting development. The unison entry of all strings is quite commonly employed as well as the duet or solo entries.

Harmonics are but rarely found in orchestral compositions, although their use in the proper places is most effective. Harmonics in quick tempi should never be essayed, but in moderate, deliberate tempo, in p or pp, a rare and spirituelle tone-color results. Harmonics are quite commonly employed in the very high register of the violins in a final cadence chord where the effect of a lingering ppp is desired. Such natural harmonics offer very little difficulty to the performer, but the young composer should not attempt to insert artificial harmonics into his work for string orchestra, as they are not always within the technical compass of the routined orchestral players. In artistic solo passages, or in the string trio or quartet, they frequently find place.

---

[1] See page 234.   [2] See page 228.

Fred. A. Stock·"C minor Quartet"

In continuing scale passages, or in shifting figures from one instrument to another, an overlapping note should always be used so that no break in the line will be discernible.

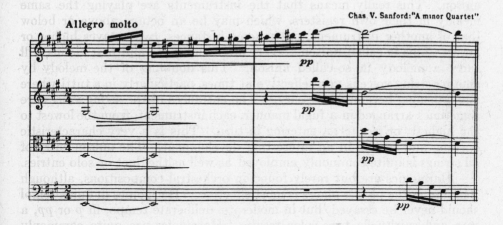

Chas. V. Sanford:"A minor Quartet"

Interlocking chords and also melodies are of frequent occurrence in writing for strings. The interlocking of chords, in the second violins and violas, is especially to be desired, as this will make for smoother tone production through this blending, as well as a more natural technic in double-stopping. The interlocking of melodies, or, in other words, the crossing of the string voices, occurs quite frequently.

Andante espressivo

Chas. V. Stanford: "A minor Quartet"

The foregoing example illustrates the interlocking of chords between the violins in the first measure. In the fourth, fifth, sixth and seventh measures the cello voice is over the viola.

Very animated

Vincent d'Indy: "E major Quartet"

Example of pizzicato tracery around a melody in the octave in the cello and second violin.

The student is advised to transcribe a number of good piano compositions for string orchestra before attempting original work. In so doing he must use his judgment in filling in chord-tones and added voices (filled voices), remembering that the latter must not be over-assertive. The intention of the composer must be faithfully considered in each transcription, and only those slight changes that become necessary through dealing with the string orchestra should be made.

The following examples of four different transcriptions of the same piano composition are given to enable the student to visualize the possibilities in arrangements of other piano works of a like character:

Clementi:"Op. 36, No. 2"

The excerpt above is arranged for string orchestra in four different ways. This is done to enable the student to gauge the possibilities of transcription.

No. I

In the foregoing arrangement the theme is given to the first violins. Double-stops are formed from the harmonies for the second violins and violas. The cellos carry the figuration, and the basses double in the lower octave with the first note of cello figure. This transcription adheres more strictly to the original than do the following arrangements, which are given to illustrate the strengthening of the melody by doubling and the addition of filled voices.

The theme is again carried in the first violins; double-stops in the second violins. Violas do the figuration. Cellos, divisi: first, doubling with the first violins in lower octave; second, doubling with the bass on the strong accent and adding pulsation note on the weak accent; basses carrying the harmonic underpinning. This example is brighter and snappier than No. I.

Theme in first violins; new figuration in second violins; original figuration in violas. Cellos, divisi: first section playing a counter-melody, while the second section plays as in No. II; double-basses the same as in No. II.

First violins, divisi, playing theme in octaves; double-stops in a new arrangement in the second violins and violas. Cellos, divisi: first section doubling with first violins in the lower octave; the second section playing the original figuration; basses playing the cello figure of No. III an octave lower. This example is to give added brightness to the general ensemble as well as a stronger rhythmic definition.

The Piccolo

The Wooden Flute

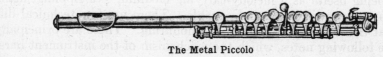

The Metal Piccolo

The Metal Flute

CHAPTER XI. THE FLUTE

Italian: *Flauto*
French: *Flûte*
German: *Flöte*

RANGE, TECHNIC, COMBINATIONS WITH THE STRINGS — EXAMPLES AND EXERCISES

The flute is the most agile instrument of the wood-wind section of the orchestra. It is capable of performing all varieties of passages, both in slow and rapid tempo, and in all varieties of tone-color from *ppp* to *fff*. The range of the modern flute is:

The two lowest semi-tones, C and C♯, are not of great use except in *f* or *ff* parts. The upper extreme, between A and C, is possible in very loud ensemble, but should be avoided, as a general rule, because of its shrillness and uncertain intonation. The top notes may be approached in scale progression but should not be held.

The flute is an instrument suggestive of all forms of ornamental passage work: musical embroideries, turns, trills, variations, coloratura, etc., as well as being useful as a melody-carrying medium, — a rippling, light-hearted saunterer, swift, sure and capable. There are few technical difficulties that the flute is incapable of surmounting. These are principally trills on the following notes, which the mechanism of the instrument bars:

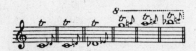

The flute combines well with the upper strings, but in certain portions of its lower register it is almost wholly lost if combined with the lower tones of the cello or any portion of the double-bass range. This is simply a question of the absorption of the overtones of the flute by the powerful overtones of the lower strings. The composer will do well to keep this in mind, particularly when writing for the flute in its lowest octave, where the quality of the tone is very expressive.

91

In strengthening the melody of the first violins it is capable and masterly, combining perfectly, and adding charm of vibration and softness of coloring to any stridency that may appear in the upper portions of the string range.   In brilliancy it is ever alert and prepossessing, inveigling snap and crispness into the melodic contour.   In florid support it is sure and easy, ornamenting with a lavish flexibility that is charming and satisfying.   In arpeggio accompaniments it is equally reliable, performing rapid skips to and fro without apparent effort.   As a consequence of these attainments in technical brilliancy, the flute is a most important factor in the general ensemble of the symphony orchestra, and its uses are almost limitless.

A List of its Important Uses

1. Sustaining notes of rather long duration.
2. Trilling notes of rather long duration, thus adding zest and energy to the general effect.
3. Doubling the melody, either in unison or an octave higher, as played on the violin, giving support and added charm of color.
4. Ornamenting the melody by use of the various figurations common to the flute.
5. Adding counterpoints or counter-melodies against the principal melody.
6. Filling in harmonic tones, adding richness to the ensemble.
7. Accompanying a simple melody by using various accompanying figures, such as arpeggios, scales, etc.
8. Ornamenting cadences.
9. Duetting with the violin or another high or medium pitched instrument.
10. Obbligatos.
11. Attacking melodies by entering with a florid flourish or scale passage on the weak part of the preceding measure.
12. Antiphonally alternating with the violin or another instrument.

Other uses for the flute will be mentioned as other instruments are added to our list, but the above twelve uses are, in the main, the important duties of the instrument.

THE PICCOLO

Italian: *Ottavino*
French: *Petite flûte*
German: *Kleine Flöte*

The miniature flute of the wood-wind section is a much smaller and shorter instrument than the flute proper.   It is higher in range, having a compass from D, on the fourth line of the treble clef, to C, two octaves and a seventh above.

The piccolo is a transposing instrument and must be written for an

octave below where it is intended to sound.

The actual notation. The sound is an octave above. This makes the piccolo the highest pitched instrument of the wood-wind section of the orchestra, and, in actual fact, except for the harmonics of the violin, the highest pitched instrument in the orchestra.

The mechanism of the piccolo is practically the same as that of the flute. Its uses in the large orchestra are rather limited, but its high, squeaky, shrill voice is useful for certain desired effects, especially in tutti passages, with the full orchestra performing in *ff* or *fff*. Its hard, whistling scale passages are familiar to all who attend symphony concerts, and its trills on high tones are very penetrating and obvious even when the full orchestra is doing its best.

It is more or less a specialized instrument in the orchestra, and usually the second flutist doubles in the piccolo when occasion demands, returning to the flute after the piccolo passage has been performed.

Its principal uses are in ornamental figures above the flute register. Here it shows off its sharp brilliancy to advantage. It is also used for exotic effects in oriental music, or may be employed for melody-doubling above the range of the flute, for which it then substitutes. Its quick scale-passage work, both up and down, makes it useful in depicting the elements when troubled by wind or storm, or its quick turning of figures may gain for it a sense of humor in a scherzo or other similar composition. The piccolo in its middle register is a fair substitute for the flute, and, in order to avoid quick interchanging of the two instruments by the same player, it may thus be used.

The orchestrator should be careful to avoid the extremes of its register, its best compass being from G on the second line of the treble clef, to G just below the top note. This, of course, sounds an octave higher than written.

A characteristic flute passage showing the ornamental use of the instrument.

Pastoral coloring illustrating the flexibility of the flute technique.

There is nothing especially brilliant in the above passage, but the quality of the flute voices is charming in this portion of the range.

EXERCISES

Trills and scale passages.

Piccolo ornamentation.

Another excellent example of flute music.

Mrs. H. H. A. Beach: "Theme and variations, Flute & String Quartet"

Andantino con morbidezza quasi valzer lento

Courtesy of G. Schirmer

Moderato con moto

Harvey Worthington Loomis:"Hark, Hark! the Lark"

Courtesy of G. Schirmer

Mendelssohn's *Songs Without Words*

Exercise I. Arrange the last twenty-four measures of No. 12 for flute and string orchestra.

Exercise II. Arrange the first eighteen measures of No. 8 for two flutes and strings.

Exercise III. Beethoven *Sonata* No. 5, Op. 10, No. 1. Beginning in measure 22, arrange to measure 45 for flute and strings.

Exercise IV. Beethoven *Sonata* No. 10, Op. 14, No. 2. Arrange the first forty-seven measures of the first movement for flute and strings.

Exercise V. Compose a short expression piece for flute and strings.

THE BASS–FLUTE

Italian: *Flauto Contralto*
French: *La Flûte Alto*
German: *Altflöte*

This instrument, which is similar in fingering and written range to the regular flute, sounds a perfect fourth lower than notated:

The music must then be written in the key a fourth higher than that in which it is to sound:

The tone-color of the bass-flute is very beautiful, especially in its middle register; and while it is less assertive than is the regular flute in the same register, it is fuller and more tender in expression.

The bottom register, from written C to A♭, is strong and sounds a great deal like a combination of viola and bassoon playing in unison.

The top tones, from written E to C, are its least useful register, being somewhat hard in tone texture, and are more favorably played by the regular flute.

The bass-flute is not considered one of the regular instruments of the orchestra, but for special coloring in some characteristic passage its solo possibilities are most gratifying.

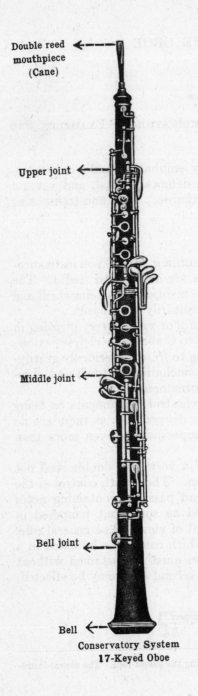

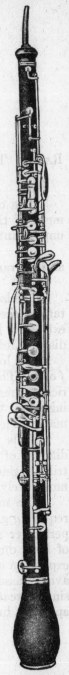

Double reed
mouthpiece
(Cane)

Upper joint

Middle joint

Bell joint

Bell

**Conservatory System
17-Keyed Oboe**

**Old System
15-Keyed Oboe**

**Modern
English Horn**

CHAPTER XII. THE OBOE

Italian: *Oboe*
French: *Hautbois*
German: *Die Hoboe*

RANGE, TECHNIC, TONE-COLOR AND COMBINATIONS — EXAMPLES AND EXERCISES

The oboe is the most characteristically emphatic wood-wind instrument of the wood-wind choir. Its tone is definitely nasal, and yet not unpleasantly so in spite of its penetrating timbre. It is non-transposing and its range is:

The lowest tones between B♭* and E, according to books on instrumentation, are weak, but in reality these tones are strong and useful. The extremely high third between C and E is also mentioned as being shrill and disagreeable, but, on the contrary, is not necessarily unpleasant.

The lowest tones, while hard to "get" in *p* or *pp*, are very pleasing in *f* or *ff*. The middle register, from first line E to C above the clef, is flexible, rich, expressive in all tonal shadings from *ppp* to *fff*, and decidedly gratifying in all varieties of technical tone figures, including diatonic and chromatic scales, arpeggios, repeated notes and ornamentations.

Trills indicated in the textbooks on orchestral instruments as being difficult of performance should be absolutely disregarded, as there are no trills within the flexible register that are impossible or even more than moderately difficult.

The mouthpiece of the oboe consists of a very thin double reed not requiring great air pressure to set in vibration. The breath control of the performer should be carefully considered, and passages containing notes of long duration or overlong phrases should be somewhat tempered in expansion and considered from a singer's point of view. As a general rule, avoid passages to be played in one breath which cannot be hummed in a single breath. When a note of long duration must be sustained without apparent break, an overlapping from first to second oboe may be effected.

* The lowest B♭ is not found on all instruments, B being the lowest tone. The newest instruments are all made with the B♭ extension.

Its uses with the other instruments of the orchestra are many and varied. Among its most important ensemble duties are:

1. Doubling with the melody-carrying instruments.

2. Carrying the melody in the wind choir.

3. Carrying counterpoint melodies against the main theme.

4. Filling in the harmonies by sustaining tones of long or short duration.

5. Certain ornamentations that are not too prominent in character may be used, but the individual tone character of the instrument should be taken into consideration, as its overpowering timbre might easily overbalance or overshadow the original intention of the composer.

6. Duetting with another wood-wind or with another instrument.

7. Obbligatos.

8. Antiphonally carrying a melody with another instrument.

9. Helping the general mass ensemble in tutti passages.

It is one of the most expressive of melodic instruments of the orchestra, and its solo possibilities are well known, especially in pastoral or nature expressions, as well as in the exotic depictions of the weird and the unusual.

EXAMPLES

Vincent d'Indy: "Bb major Symphony"

The oboe doubled in the lower octave with the flute. The oboe, while not appearing to great advantage there, assists materially in the ensemble.

Richard Strauss: "From Italy"

Illustrating the topmost register of the instrument.

Saint Saens "Cello Concerto in A minor"

This figure is repeated a major third higher after a rest of one measure. Simple and effective scoring for oboe.

Claude A. Debussy "La Mer"

Leo Delibes "Sylvia"

The above is a simple appearing little passage, but quite difficult because of the staccato notes which seem quite evasive in this particular example.

Liszt "Hungarian Rhapsodie No 2"

Characteristic oboe music.

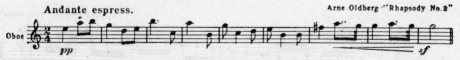

Arne Oldberg "Rhapsody No. 2"

For other examples of oboe uses, see pages 214 to 245.

THE ENGLISH HORN

Italian: *Corno inglese*
French: *Cor anglais*
German: *Englisches Horn*

RANGE, TONE-COLOR, COMBINATIONS — EXAMPLES — EXERCISES

The English horn is neither a horn nor English. It is a wood-wind instrument of the oboe type of construction, resembling it in form, though somewhat larger, and having a differently shaped and more pronounced bell. The technic of the English horn is practically the same as is that of the oboe, and, in fact, the instrument might be classed as an alto oboe. It is a transposing instrument sounding a perfect fifth lower than the notation, and consequently should be written for in the key a perfect fifth higher than the original key of the composition in which it is employed. The written range is, except for the low B♭, the same as that of the oboe. The G, or treble, clef is always used.

The general effect of the tone-color of the English horn is sorrowful, mysterious, weird and sometimes grotesque. Its combination with other instruments of the orchestra is neither gratifying nor especially useful, as its quantity and quality of tone are practically negligible in ensemble, except where a soft but very "reedy" tone effect is particularly desired.

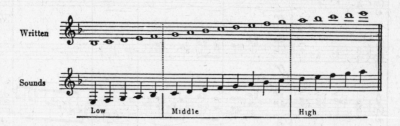

The low register is rather expressionless and unpleasant whether in *f* or *p*. The middle register is the most useful. The high register is somewhat the same as the middle register of the oboe without its fullness or brilliance. The English horn is a specialized instrument and should be used only for certain definite effects, and not as a generally accepted orchestral factor. Except for the bizarre purposes expected of it, other instruments regularly employed in the orchestra and having the same range may be utilized to better advantage in the way of filling in, doubling or strengthening. It is, all in all, a sinister, mysterious sounding oboe in low-pitched range.

The second oboist usually is expected to change to the English horn when a passage for the latter instrument is introduced into the composition, unless a decided prominence is given to the part, in which case two oboes and English horn should be indicated in the scoring.

EXAMPLES

Mendelssohn's *Songs Without Words*

Exercise I. Arrange the first sixteen measures of No. 20 for oboe solo and strings.

Exercise II. Arrange the last ten measures of No. 18 for flute, English horn and strings.

Exercise III. Arrange the last eighteen measures of No. 3 for piccolo, flute (octave below) and necessary strings.

Exercise IV. Beethoven *Sonata* No. 11, Op. 22. Arrange first thirty measures of the adagio for flute, oboe and strings.

Exercise V. Beethoven *Sonata*, Op. 2, No. 3. Arrange the last thirty-eight measures of the final movement for flute, oboe and string orchestra.

Exercise VI. Compose a short expression piece for piccolo, flute, oboe, English horn and strings.

For examples of English horn technic, see pages 217, 219, 224, 226, 231, 232.

Single reed mouthpiece ←

Bell ←

Bb or A Clarinet
Boehm System

Bb Bass Clarinet

Bb or A Clarinet
Albert System

The Clarinet Family

CHAPTER XIII. THE CLARINET

Italian: *Clarinetto*
French: *Clarinette*
German: *Klarinette*

RANGE, TECHNIC, TONE-COLOR, USES AND CHARACTER — EXAMPLES AND
EXERCISES

Were one to inquire of an orchestral conductor of experience which
one of the wood-wind instruments was indispensable should he be obliged
to rearrange his orchestra to strings, one wood-wind, horns, trumpets, etc.,
it is almost certain that, from the viewpoint of all-around usefulness, he
would insist that the clarinet be allowed to remain.

The importance of the clarinet in the modern orchestra is far greater
than any other single wood-wind, in that its range, overlapping into that
of the bassoon, covering practically all the sphere of action of the English
horn and oboe, and encroaching favorably into the highest tones of the
flute, gives to it a very wide and defined field of activity.

The composer has to consider two important things in connection with
the instrument: (1) transposition and (2) signature.

The two clarinets universally employed are tuned in A major and B♭
major. That in A sounds a minor third lower than written, the B♭ a major
second lower. Consequently he must change the original signature of the
composition to meet the requirements of the instrument which he is to use.

The second consideration, the signature, will determine which of the
two clarinets he should use.   A general rule seems to indicate that he employ
the A clarinet for sharp keys and the B♭ clarinet for flat keys.   This will
work out practically most of the time, and for the present this will be
permitted to stand.

The written range of the clarinet is:

This gives to the instrument a working compass of three octaves and
a fifth.

The A clarinet, sounding a minor third lower than the notation, has

the following range: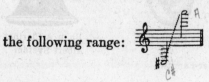

The B♭ clarinet, sounding a major second lower than the notation, has the following range:

There has been much controversy in regard to the actual difference in quality of sound between the A and B♭ clarinets. The A clarinet was considered less bright and crisp than the B♭ clarinet, but in actual fact there is little, if any, difference in quality between the two. Abandoning, then, the idea of choosing the clarinet because of its tone-color, the one consideration remaining in the matter of choice rests entirely with the key of the composition. A choice should be made involving the fewest number of accidentals in the clarinet signature, thus simplifying the technic for the performer.

For sharp keys use the A clarinet, subtracting the three sharps of the instrument from the signature. Thus, if the composition is in four sharps, E major or C♯ minor, the signature for the clarinet will be one sharp, — G major or E minor. If the signature of the composition has fewer sharps than the A clarinet, add flats for the missing sharps. Thus, if the composition is in two sharps, D major or B minor, the signature for the clarinet will be one flat, — F major or D minor.

Sound desired

A clarinet

B♭ clarinet.   Note the number of sharps involved

For flat keys use the B♭ clarinet, subtracting the two flats of the instrument from the signature.

Thus, if the composition is in E♭ major or C minor, the signature for the clarinet will be one flat, — F major or D minor. If the signature has fewer flats than the clarinet, add sharps for the missing flats. Thus, if the composition is in C major or A minor (two flats less than the clarinet), the signature for the clarinet will be two sharps, — D major or B minor.

Sound desired

B♭ clarinet

A clarinet.   Note the flats in the signature

A good general rule to follow is:

For compositions in sharp keys write the signature of the key a minor third higher and the notation a minor third higher, using the A clarinet.

For compositions in flat keys write the signature of the key a major second higher and the notation a major second higher, using the B♭ clarinet.

Where a lengthy composition involving a number of modulations to distant keys is to be considered, the composer should not attempt to change from one clarinet to the other to meet the requirements above stated, but should choose the clarinet which will be best suited for the greater part of the composition, and then for the involved modulations help the performer either by enharmonic changes of key or through notation in the original key with the necessary accidentals placed before the notes of those passages.

Example. — Composition in A♭ major; modulations of importance to F♯ major, A major, D♭, B♭; return to A♭.

The B♭ clarinet should be used in signature of B♭ sounding in key of A♭.

First modulation to F♯ major should be enharmonically changed to G♭ and written in the signature of A♭ (four flats).

Second modulation to A major should be in the signature of B (five sharps), and if not too lengthy a passage should simply be "accidentalled." If the modulation is lengthy, the A clarinet may be resorted to, provided an opportunity for the change from the B♭ clarinet (several measures) is granted. Signature for A clarinet, C major.

Third modulation to D♭ will find the B♭ clarinet playing notes in signature of E♭ (three flats) sounding D♭.

Fourth modulation to B♭, signature C major.

Return to A♭, signature B♭.

It must be stated that the clarinetist in the modern orchestra has grown with the natural trend of the times, and his technical skill has kept pace with all the requirements expected of him in the compositions of such men as Strauss, d'Indy, Schoenberg and others. The matter of keys is a matter of technic, and the orchestrator should turn his attention to the elimination of as much of the signature as is possible and consistent with the effect desired. Before deciding which clarinet he will use, he should study the composition from the angle of its various tonal changes. Upon summing up he will readily determine which instrument or instruments to employ. He should remember that it is poor policy to change clarinets during the progress of a composition unless it becomes absolutely necessary to do so; and when such a change is made, he must remember that the performer is leaving his warm reed for a cold reed and should be permitted several measures' leeway for preparation.

There are very few technical impossibilities to be recorded for the composer to observe. Certain trills should be avoided when the instrument is in prominent display, but may be used in tutti passages. These are:

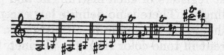

There are four weak tones on the instrument which should be observed:

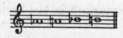

These are difficult to manage and should be avoided in any variety of passage work, such as tremolos, trills, figuration of chord-tones, repeated or tongued notes, notes of skips, etc. These tones may be freely employed in tutti, especially if doubled with another instrument; but in solo or any prominent melody work they should be given to another instrument to perform.

The clarinet exhibits singular power and resonance in its lowest or "Chalumeau" register:

These tones are intensely colorful and are useful in a variety of effects, either in solo or ensemble. The following register is weak:

As was stated, these tones are weak, insecure and likely to be faulty in intonation.

Now follows the real clarinet quality and the characteristically beautiful register of the instrument which can be absolutely relied upon in all tone-shades from *pp* to *ff* and in all varieties of technic from diatonic scale passage to chromatic or arpeggic figuration. There seem to be no impossible musical inventions of melody that the clarinet is incapable of mastering in the following register:

The top tones, from A♭ to C, are piercing in quality and are best avoided, especially as they are very difficult of production.

In considering the clarinet in ensemble with the flute and oboe, it is well to note the best registers of each instrument and permit interlocking of harmonies accordingly. There is no definite law except that of attention to effect, and this should be the guide in all instances. Even though the oboe is widely different in tone-color from the clarinet, the student should have no fear in combining the two instruments in ensemble passage work, permitting them to alternate one above the other in the sustaining of filled harmonic tones.

A list of the uses of the clarinet in the orchestra follows:

1. Melody carrying.

2. Variations around the melody.

3. Doubling the melody with flute or oboe or violins, or, possibly, the viola.

4. Scale passages, either legato or staccato.

5. Arpeggios.

6. Long skips. Avoid the octave skips in repetition in fast work; all others are good.

7. Filling in of sustained tones in the harmony against passage work in other instruments.

8. Tremolos of intervals of thirds, fourths and fifths not involving C♯ nor crossing or including the middle register notes.

9. Double-noting and triple-noting except on weak notes indicated.

10. Antiphonal uses.

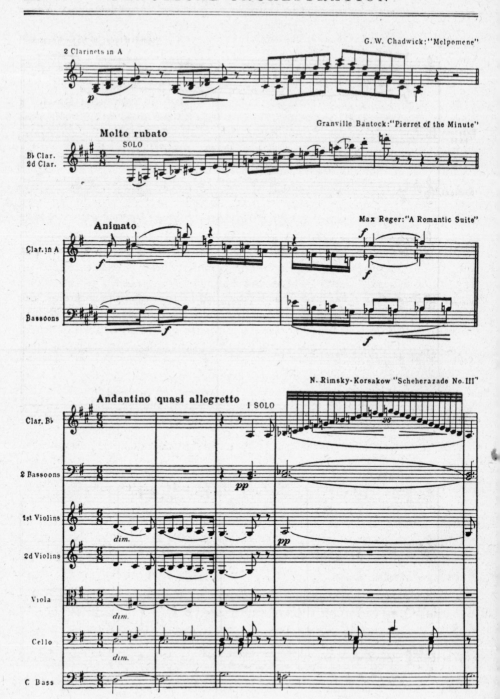

Vincent d'Indy:"B♭ Major Symphony"

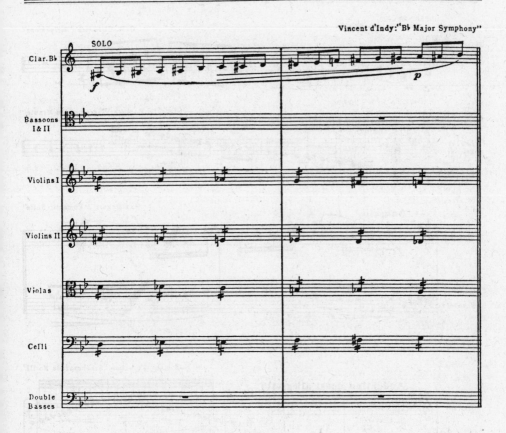

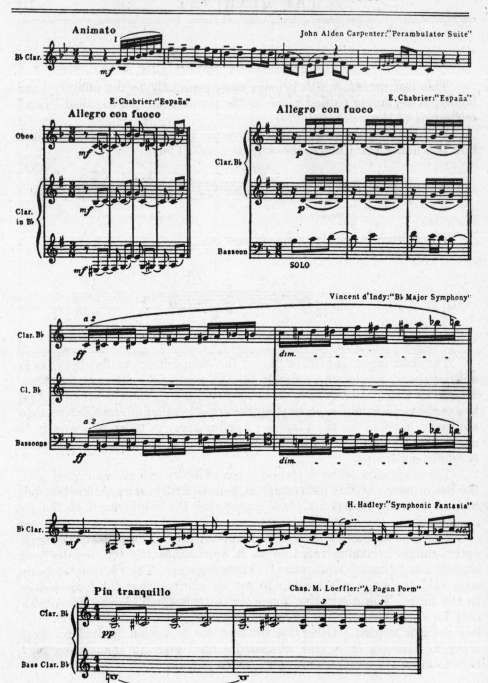

For further study of clarinet technic, see pages 214 to 245.

THE E♭ CLARINET

This instrument, which belongs more especially to the military band family, is beginning to find place in the regular and the so-called "jazz" orchestras of the present day.

In pitch it is a perfect fourth above the B♭ clarinet, and its transposition is a minor third above the written note. Thus:

Written   Sound

The written range of the E♭ clarinet is:

Written   Sound

The instrument is best employed for compositions in flat keys, as in military band music where nearly all the music is written in flat keys. When the transpositions involve sharp keys, the signatures at once begin to assume proportions necessitating the consideration of more sharps than are easily handled by the players. For instance, in order to sound in G major the E♭ clarinet must read in four sharps; D major, five sharps; A major, six sharps.

There appears to be a certain sense of awkwardness connected with the performance of this instrument in keys of many sharps, and it is well to bear in mind this point when considering the employment of the E♭ clarinet in the scoring for orchestra.

The tone of the E♭ clarinet is hard, brittle and shrill throughout its entire range, becoming more so as it approaches the top register and slightly less "glassy" as it nears its lower register. The E♭ clarinet bears somewhat the same relationship to the B♭ clarinet that the piccolo does to the flute. The distinctive tone-color of this small clarinet is suitable only for ensemble purposes where its brittle staccato or shrieking, timbreless voice is needed. Otherwise its uses are somewhat limited to short arpeggio passages or figures wherein its hard piercing enunciation may help to fill out a tempestuous entry into a climax.

See page 224.

CHAPTER XIV. THE BASS CLARINET

Italian: *Clarinetto basso*
French: *Clarinette basse*
German: *Bass Klarinette*

The bass clarinet, of which there is but one,* tuned in B♭, is exactly an octave lower than the regular B♭ clarinet, and consequently its range is:

The actual sound of this range is an octave and a major second lower than the notation:

There are two methods of notation which the student should understand. The French notation, which is universally employed, is that indicated on the treble, or G, clef, the sound being an octave and a whole tone deeper; and the German notation, which is on the bass, or F, clef, the sound being a whole tone lower.

French notation

German notation

Sound

The instrument is of the same construction as the ordinary clarinet, although longer, the bell-joint being curved upward and outward before flaring into a slightly wider opening than that of the regular clarinet. The fingering of the bass clarinet is the same as that of the smaller instrument.

---

* There were formerly three bass clarinets, tuned in C, A and B♭. That in C sounded one octave lower than notated; that in A, an octave and a minor third lower. The B♭ bass clarinet alone remains in use.

All that has been said concerning the weak tones, trills, etc., of the regular clarinet is applicable to the bass clarinet, and should be observed by the student. The instrument is far from satisfactory in the way of color. Its entire tonal range is hollow-sounding, breathy and inclined to be unpleasant. Legato passages are its best medium of expression. Sombre effects can be realized, but bravura work should be given to other deep-pitched instruments, as, when performed upon the bass clarinet, it is lacking in rhythmic precision and contorted in such a way as to be almost grotesque. Consequently, as with the English horn, we are again dealing with a specialized instrument which finds but little regular orthodox use in the average orchestra. The modern composer finds place for it in special effects of gray colors, as might be expected in compositions depicting sorrow, death, pain or torture; or, again, in attempting to define the strange or exotic, or the grotesque, as in burlesquing.

It may also be used for sustained bass doublings, harmonic backgrounds or for assisting in orchestral tutti where *ff* or *fff* passages require all that is possible in the orchestral body of tone.

Edward Elgar:"A♭ major Symphony"

Chas. M. Loeffler:"La Villanelle du Diable"

John Alden Carpenter: "Perambulator Suite"

Tempo di Valse

Bass Clar. B♭

H. Hadley: "Symphonic Fantasia"

Mosso agitato

Bass Clar.

G. W. Chadwick: "Euterpe" Concert Overture

Lento

Bass Clar.

Mendelssohn's *Songs Without Words*

Exercise I. Arrange the first sixteen measures of No. 38 for flute, clarinet and strings.

Exercise II. Arrange No. 49 for flute, oboe, clarinet and strings.

Exercise III. Beethoven *Sonata* No. 8, Op. 13. Arrange the last twenty-four measures of the Rondo for flute, oboe, clarinet and strings.

Exercise IV. Beethoven *Sonata* No. 13, Op. 27, No. 1. Arrange the last thirty measures for flute, oboe, clarinet, bass clarinet and strings.

Exercise V. Compose a short composition for wood-winds and strings.

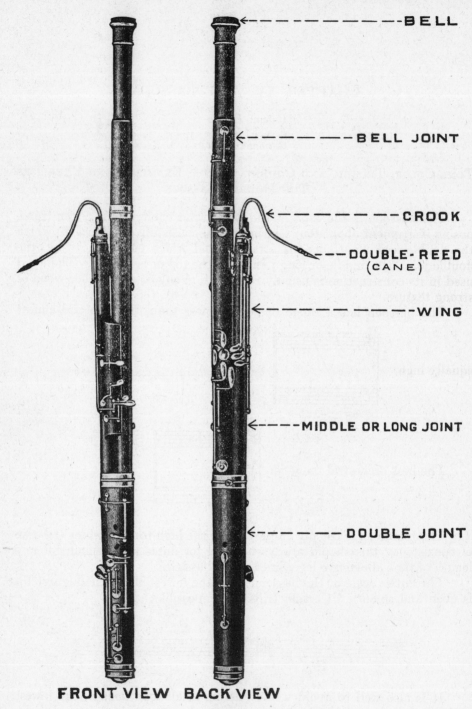

BELL

BELL JOINT

CROOK

DOUBLE-REED
(CANE)

WING

MIDDLE OR LONG JOINT

DOUBLE JOINT

FRONT VIEW   BACK VIEW

The Bassoon

CHAPTER XV. THE BASSOON

Italian: *Fagotto*
French: *Basson*
German: *Fagott*

TONE-COLOR, TECHNIC AND COMBINATIONS — EXAMPLES AND EXERCISES — THE DOUBLE–BASSOON

The bassoon is the cello of the wood-wind choir. It is a non-transposing instrument about four feet in length, consisting of a crook to which the double-reed mouthpiece is attached and which enters the wing, the double joint, the middle or long joint, and the top or bell joint. The wood used in its construction is usually rosewood, ebony or some other wood of strong texture.

The bassoon has a range one tone lower than the cello and almost

equally high.

The best orchestral range is:

The tenor clef is usually employed for the high tones, and for the sake of consistency this should always be used for notes that remain for any length of time above two leger lines of the bass clef.

The entire scale of the bassoon from the lowest B♭ to the highest B♭ is even and smooth. Certain trills are impossible:

It is also well to avoid whole-tone and half-tone trills in the lowest register of the bassoon, as these are very prominent and obtrusive. Whole-tone trills may be performed on [musical notation] and half-tone

trills on [musical notation] Because of their ungainly character they are not often employed.

This trill is possible only by having first bassoon player do the trill with his free hand on the second bassoon.

The bassoon is a masterful exponent of all varieties of tone-color throughout its entire range, and is capable of depicting emotions of every desirable nature, from humor to the most stately melodic offering. Its technical equipment is such that one need not fear writing too difficult a scale or arpeggic passage, and as an instrument of assistance in ensemble its blending and merging into the colors of the other instruments, whether string, wood-wind or brass, is everything that can be desired.

We cannot recommend it for tremolo legato, but even in such requirements it is not incapable if the composer restricts himself to intervals of thirds, either major or minor, and always above the second space of the bass clef. In full orchestra where such technical effects are used, the rest of the orchestra will help cover the production of tone and unify it into the general mass.

The instrument exhibits but few antipathies in its tonal associations with other tone mediums. In the hands of an expert performer there is little to be feared. The top tones of the orchestral range, while smooth and even, are somewhat lacking in depth of overtone color, and should be doubled in another instrument, either cello, clarinet or horn, or be surrounded by light passage figures in another accompanying wood-wind.

For staccato work the bassoon has no peer. It seems endowed with a special facility for dry, humorous passage work that is inimitable. It is gloomy in the extreme when so desired. It is dancingly exuberant when such expression is demanded. It is joyful and laughing or gruesome and "macabre-like," according to the whim of the recorder. It is an instrument of a thousand moods and uses, and consequently is a powerful factor in the orchestra.

For different manners of technic for the bassoon, see pages 214, 215, 217, 220, 221, 222, 223, 224, 225, 227, 230, 231, 232, 233, 234, 235.

EXAMPLES OF DIFFICULTIES

In the above example the bassoon cannot possibly gradate its tone-color down to *ppppp* in its low register. These four notes should be given to the bass clarinet.

In this example the staccato notes are very difficult in fast tempo, especially in the high register.

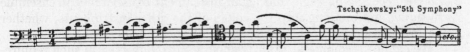

The above is a very difficult bit because of the involved phrasing.

This is also difficult because of staccato in the high register in quick tempo.

This example illustrates a difficult passage in the top register of the bassoon. The Italian instrument has these high notes, but the tones should be avoided or assigned to another wood-wind instrument.

This is another difficult staccato passage in the high register.

EXAMPLES

Characteristic measures for bassoons.

Illustrating the overlapping notes in connecting a passage through several instruments.

A cadenza for bassoon.

THE DOUBLE–BASSOON

Italian: *Contrafagotto*
French: *Contre-Basson*
German: *Kontrafagott*

The double-bassoon is the double-bass of the wood-winds. Like the double-bass, it sounds an octave lower than the notation, but, unlike the double-bass, it has few uses in the orchestra. It is ponderous, slow acting technically, heavy in textural color, raw in enunciation and altogether specialized in usefulness. It emits a gruesome tone in its lowest register, a rather awkward sonority in its middle register, and a poor imitation of the bassoon in its upper register, which ordinarily should be allotted to the more favorable instrument.

The written compass of the double-bassoon is:

In considering the uses of the double-bassoon one is limited to decidedly few definite opportunities. It is all-powerful and expressive in its proper place, but, like the unfortunate bull in the china shop, it is not welcome where it does not belong. It carries down the range of the bassoon when that is necessary; it doubles with the bass in *ff* or *fff* when the extra sonorousness is required; it plays a bit of gruesome melody in a way no other instrument can imitate when such an effect is demanded; and it supports the wood-wind choir admirably in notes of sustained duration. Quick passage work, other than moderately short scale figures or easy arpeggios, should not be essayed unless well "covered" by a full orchestra, as the result will not be as smooth or as properly ornamental as could be desired. In its proper place the double-bassoon is most effective and useful, but the instrument should be used with care and great discrimination.

EXAMPLES

THE STRINGS AND WOOD-WINDS

In working out combinations of strings and wood-winds the student will observe that the greater portion of his work will be in the balances, that is, in which registers of the instruments he must double in unison or octave with other instruments. He now has two complete, full-voiced choirs at his disposal, both capable in themselves of independence of expression, and yet each relying on the other for strength, fullness, variety of color and heightened expression.

The flute and the violin sing well together throughout their combined ranges, their colors unifying, the flute gaining in power in its lowest and medium registers, and in brilliancy and definition in its upper register. They combine excellently in the octave, but the flute should be the upper voice of the octave except in special instances.

The oboe also combines well with the violin in all registers, its peculiar tone quality becoming less defined in the unison. The lower register of the oboe gains in roundness, while the upper portion of its range becomes clearer and yet less nasal.

The clarinets combine well with violins, violas and cellos. The length of the clarinet range offers opportunities for combinations with all three of these strings. In its lowest register the cello gives to it a richness of tone-color and an added strength not possible in its combination with any other instrument. The middle register of the clarinet, when combined with the viola, gains thereby, but not to the same extent that its association with the cello produces. The union of violin and clarinet in its high register is favorable, but should be tempered with caution, as the strength of the clarinet tones can be very overpowering to the stringed instrument. Several violins are necessary to create an even balance when a unison is to be sung in the upper registers of these instruments. In its own family the clarinet combines well with the flute, the oboe, and the upper register of the bassoon.

The English horn is a special color in itself, and serves more successfully in projecting its own song than in combining with other instruments. In range it is closely related to the viola, but the combination of these two dark, sombre voices of the orchestra serves only to add further gloom to the general effect. The combination of the upper register of the cello with the English horn is somewhat better; but if a doubling of the voices is necessary it had much better be with another wood-wind voice, preferably the oboe or bassoon.

The bass clarinet is another voice quite apart from the others in tonal expression. It is more nearly related to the cello in range, although encroaching favorably into that of the viola. However, a doubling of either of these strings with the bass clarinet only adds to a general broadening of the same color value, adding neither brilliance nor definition of line. Its doubling had better be accomplished in its own family, either with the lower tones of the clarinet or the entire range of the bassoon. The deepest register of the bass clarinet is more flexible in tonal variation than is that of the bassoon, and consequently in *pp* or *ppp* effects the preference should be in favor of the bass clarinet.

The bassoon has about the same range as the cello and is one of the best "mixers" in the entire orchestra. This instrument gives virility to the other voices, especially to the cello in strengthening the bass line. It often carries the bass melody an octave higher with the double-basses, and serves in its own family as the underpinning of the choir. In its combination with the viola it assists more in brightening that instrument's vocal enunciation than does any other voice in the orchestra. Its uses are in doubling or strengthening melodies, in adding harmonic tones, in counter-melodies and in solo passages, all of which give to the bassoon an importance in the general ensemble of the large orchestra second to none.

The double-bassoon plays its few notes here and there either as a short solo or as a doubling in the lower octave with the bassoons. Its general uses are limited to carrying down the wood-wind bass line below the range of the bassoon, the doubling with the double-basses in a tutti, and the sustaining of a pedal tone for the wood-wind section in a wood-wind tutti.

The following various combinations are often encountered in studying scores:

1. Flute and strings: flute in unison or higher octave with first violins.

2. Flute, two clarinets and strings: flute in unison or higher octave with first violins; first clarinet in unison with violins, second clarinet doubling with alto voice.

3. Flute, oboe, two clarinets and strings: flute either doubling in higher octave with first violins and violas or filling in; oboe doubling in unison with the first violins or adding counter-melodies; clarinets doubling and filling.

4. Flute, oboe, two clarinets, bassoon and strings: the same as No. 3, except that the bassoon doubles in the bass line with cellos.

5. Two flutes, oboe, two clarinets, bassoon and strings: various combinations.

6. Two flutes, two oboes, two clarinets, two bassoons and strings: general doubling throughout.

7. Two flutes, piccolo, two oboes, two clarinets, bass clarinet, two bassoons and strings.

8. Three flutes (one interchangeable with piccolo), two oboes, English horn, two clarinets, bass clarinet, two bassoons, double-bassoon and strings.

In scoring for these instruments the wood-winds should be written at the top of the score-page in the following order:

> Two flutes, one piccolo
> > or
> One piccolo, two flutes.
> Two oboes.
> One English horn.
> Two clarinets in B♭ or A.
> One bass clarinet in B♭.
> Two bassoons.
> Double-bassoon.
> First violins.
> Second violins.
> Violas.
> Cellos.
> Double-basses.

The two flutes are written on one staff. The piccolo, which may be written above or below the flutes, should occupy a staff by itself, except when it is interchangeable with a third flute.

The two oboes occupy one staff. The English horn, which is transposing and consequently has a different signature from the other wood-winds, should have its own staff.

The clarinets have one staff; the bass clarinet, one staff. The two bassoons are written on one staff; and the double-bassoon, which is sometimes interchangeable with a third bassoon, has its own staff.

If any instrument or instruments are omitted in the scoring, the general order of arrangement is not affected except as to the omission of these instruments.

See pages 214, 215, 217, 219, 220, 221, 222, 223, 224, 225, 227, 228, 229, 230, 231, 235, 242, 243 for various combinations.

EXAMPLE

Mendelssohn's *Songs Without Words*

Exercise I. Arrange the first sixteen measures of No. 48 for woodwinds.

Exercise II. Arrange the first sixteen measures of No. 35 for woodwinds.

Exercise III. Beethoven *Sonata* No. 7, Op. 10, No. 3. Arrange the first forty-eight measures of the largo for flute, oboe, English horn, clarinets, bass clarinet, bassoons and double-bassoon.

Exercise IV. Beethoven *Sonata* No. 8, Op. 13. Arrange the introduction, grave, for wood-winds and strings.

Exercise V. Compose a short sketch for wood-winds and strings, including all the instruments thus far studied, with the exception of the viola d'amour.

CHAPTER XVI. THE HUNTING-HORN

French: *Cor de chasse*

So much praise has been bestowed upon the hunting-horn because of its richness and beauty of tone that a few words regarding it seem necessary before taking up the study of the valve-horn. The hunting-horn formerly consisted of a long tube twisted spirally into close folds and gradually expanding from the cupped, funneled mouthpiece to the flaring bell. The instrument produced tones that were the natural result of the partials of the keynote in which the horn itself was pitched. These partials, or natural tones, comprised a range of three octaves:

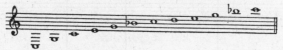

All compositions, or horn-calls, were based on this harmonic series, and it was not until the latter part of the sixteenth century that the instrument became a factor in the orchestra.

Developments, meanwhile, had taken place, and by means of stopping the instrument by inserting the hand into the bell, some of the intermediate tones between those of the harmonic series gave it a more or less diatonic as well as a partial chromatic scale. Further improvements brought about through the invention of "crooks" — neatly coiled brass tubing of various lengths — enabled the player to change the harmonic series to comply more or less with the signature of the music being performed. Thus we find in the compositions of the old masters score indications reading, Horn in C, Horn in G, Horn in E♭, etc., but all written in the key of C. This, automatically, made the horn a transposing instrument; for while the performer always read his notes in C, the crook caused them to sound in the key indicated by the composer. We find that of the sixteen different tunings made possible through the employment of the crooks, as well as through a later invention called the slide, several soon fell into disuse, leaving the following tunings: B♭, C, D, E, E♭, F, G, A♭, A and B♭ alto.

But still the horn could not comply with all the requirements of the ever-expanding demands of the composer; and even though he complied, to the best of his ability, with the uneven scale and the several missing tones, as well as with the uncertainties of pitch, there remained a great deal to be desired. Open tones were generally to be relied upon to produce the effect desired; but the stopped tones changed not only color of tone, but were at times very shaky in pitch, thus creating variations not at all intended.

These circumstances caused experimentation which resulted in the invention of valves, which, while somewhat lessening the beauty of tone of the instrument, gave to it an evenness of scale both diatonic and chromatic, as well as a flexibility of technic in its entire compass never before attainable. Thus the horn becomes a most impressive and important factor in the modern orchestra.

THE FRENCH HORN OR THE VALVE-HORN

French: *Cor-a-pistons*
Italian: *Corno a machina*
German: *Ventilhorn*

RANGE, TECHNIC, TONE-COLOR, USES AND COMBINATIONS — EXAMPLES — EXERCISES

It is only in recent years that the question of which horn to use in the scoring of a composition has resolved itself into practically no choice at all; for no matter which horn the composer indicates, the player will employ but one horn, that in F, which seems to be the universally accepted instrument of the formerly large horn family. It is the survival of the fittest; for undoubtedly the F horn is the most useful, as well as the best mannered, of the ten horns that the player, as well as the composer, was forced to rack his brains over in former times.

A short résumé of the horns formerly employed in the orchestra will be of great assistance to the student in the matter of score reading, and is herewith given.

Horn in B♭ basso

Actual sound a major ninth lower

All diatonic and chromatic notes between the given open or natural tones are playable by using the valves. The smoothest and most favorable range is bracketed. This horn is powerful and rich.

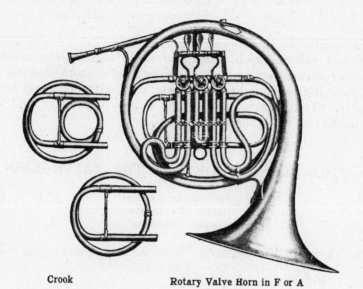

Crook   Rotary Valve Horn in F or A

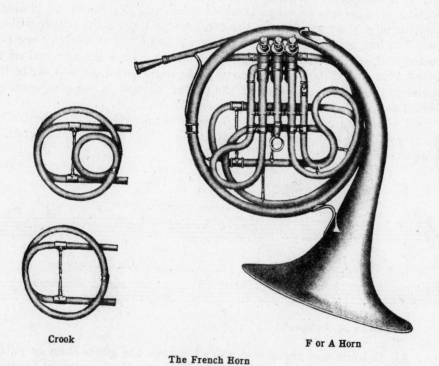

Crook   F or A Horn

The French Horn

Almost like the B♭ basso horn in color, but slightly harsher.

Less full than the B♭ or C horns, with softer, slightly veiled color.

The E♭ horn is like the D horn in tone-color, but is less veiled.

The E horn is tender, full and very expressive in color, approaching nearer the quality of the F horn than any of the other instruments.

Horn in F

Sound a perfect fifth lower.

The F horn has a full, noble, clear, rich quality of tone.

Horn in G

Sound a perfect fourth lower

The G horn has a sharper and more penetrating tone than the F horn.

Horn in A♭

Sound a major third lower

The A♭ horn, while also penetrating in tone, is less harsh than the G horn.

Horn in A

Sound a minor third lower

The A horn is much the same timbre as the G horn, sharp and penetrating.

B♭ alto horn

Sound a major second lower

The B♭ alto horn is the harshest and shrillest of the horn family.

The student should note that the written range for all horns is the same, *i.e.*, from C on the second space of the bass clef up three octaves. These notes are all playable, but the most flexible register, where the fewest technical difficulties occur, is between the two bracketed Gs.

It will be observed from the given illustrations that the horns were pitched in the various commonly used keys, and that the signature of the composition influenced the choice of horn to be employed. Thus all the horn parts were written in C major and sounded in the key of the composition. The horns were also classified as to pitch:

High-pitched horns:	Medium-pitched horns:	Low-pitched horns:
B♭ alto horn.	F horn.	D horn.
A horn.	E horn.	C horn.
A♭ horn.	E♭ horn.	B♭ basso horn.
G horn.		

Of these, the B♭ basso, the E, the F and the A horns seem to be the most practical from the viewpoint of good tonal results, the others being harsh, veiled, sharp, penetrating or depressed. Especially so was the B♭ alto horn, which boasted the hardest and sharpest tones of the large unruly family.

The B♭ basso horn has a full, powerful tone.

The E horn has a clear, tender, full tone.

The F horn has a noble, full, rich quality of tone surpassing all the others in variety and charm.

The A horn has a rather sharp, penetrating tone.

The F horn, which will now receive our undivided attention, has a

sounding range:

including all diatonic and chromatic tones. To this may be added the

following low pedal tones, which are occasionally used:

In writing for the F horn, the treble or G clef is used except for deep passages, where the bass clef is occasionally requisitioned in order to facilitate reading.

Formerly the rather stupid system of writing the horn parts on the bass clef an octave lower than was actually intended was in vogue, and a great many of the early scores still exhibit this ancient manner of notation; but the present bass notation is very definite in regard to the actual transposition.

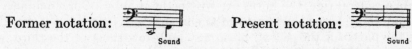

The smoothest range, both in regard to evenness of scale and tech-

nical flexibility is: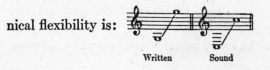

The tones below this range,  while possible, are

slightly more difficult of production, and those in the extremely high

register 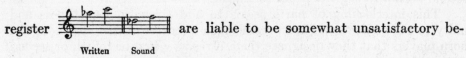 are liable to be somewhat unsatisfactory be-

cause of the technical demands on the lips of the player, as well as the resourcefulness of breath control required of him.

The horn, in its warmth and nobility of tone, is neither brass nor wood-wind in character. It is not tinged with the ever-present feeling of brassiness that one distinguishes as a characteristic feature of the other instruments of the brass section; and as a consequence of this, its possibilities of blending with and melting into the tones of the other instruments of the orchestra are so great as to make it the most valuable and most useful instrument of the brass choir.

No other brass instrument can give to solo passages the charm and nobleness that the horn expresses. For accompanying purposes its color lends interest through its blending powers already mentioned. As a background of harmonies, it is as important a success as in its other uses. Its adaptability to the spirit of the expression involved places the horn in a class by itself, and demands of the composer a very deep and conscientious study of its technical handling in its various phases, the tone-color in its entire register, its phrasing as regards breath control, its muted, muffled and stopped significances, its uses with other instruments and its uses in ornamentation.

The composer may employ two, three or four horns (usually a quartet of horns in the average large orchestra), and they are designated first, second, third and fourth horns. The first horn is generally expected to play the allotted solos, although to any one of the four horns may be assigned this mark of distinction.

As a general rule, the horns are written in an interlocking manner, the first and third horns duetting and the second and fourth horns duetting. Thus the parts for the second horn may lie below those of the third horn a great deal of the time. In fact, the first and third horns are considered the "high" horns, and the second and fourth the "low" horns.

The first and third horns, then, will be expected to perform between [music] while the second and fourth horns perform between

[music] The fourth hornist specializes on the pedal tones, which

are performed with a very loose embouchure. [music] The second horn also is given pedal tones.

This interlocking of parts seems to add strength, smoothness and unity to the quartet, and has become such a matter of custom among the horn players that they designate themselves as a first or fourth or second or third hornist, and prefer the positions to which they have been trained.

R. Wagner: "Meistersinger"

In the foregoing excerpt from Wagner's *Meistersinger*, it will be noted that in measure one the second horn is sounding below the third horn, and again, at the end of measure four, the second horn will be found below the third. This is very frequently the case in writing for the horn quartet. It should also be noted in this illustration that the horns are quite widely dispersed or separated, covering at times a range of over two octaves.

No signature is employed in writing for the horns, and as a consequence the proper accidentals should be carefully inscribed in the music.

The F horn sounds in the key of F major, and if "F" is written and played, the sound emitted will be B♭, a perfect fifth below:

Therefore parts for the F horn must be written a perfect fifth higher than the key signature of the original composition.

Thus to notate the following melody

it should be written a perfect fifth higher, and the flats in the signature, as well as the accidentals introduced, should be indicated by accidentals in the horn part.

The various rhythmic figures which are not difficult of execution on the horn comprise diatonic and chromatic scales in fast or slow tempo, and in staccato or legato enunciation. Thus a passage such as the following offers no difficulties to the player:

Arpeggic figures in the following manner are also playable:

In fact, all varieties of major, minor and diminished triads and sevenths

arranged into arpeggios within the smooth range   are play-

able either staccato or legato in not too rapid tempi.

Repeated notes, if not too rapid or through too many measures, are not difficult, but it should be borne in mind that the performer must breathe from time to time; consequently, proper phrasing, just as though one were writing for the voice, must be considered and indicated. Figures such as the following are often met with in music for the horn:

Ornamentation is usually a matter of concern for the performer unless written within the instrument's most facile range. Whole-tone trills are performed with the lips, and are best written between ♯ for the F horn. There are other whole-tone trills which might be indicated, but which in reality are "fictitious" or "trick" trills, and are not playable by all hornists, and as a consequence do not find place in the technic of the most serious performers. Half-tone trills are playable from and require the use of the valve.

Grace notes, turns and simple ornamentations within this same range are easily played, but should be avoided in the extreme registers.

The muting of the horn is usually accomplished by inserting the hand into the bell of the instrument. This is called stopping the tones, and is indicated in the music by the mark + over the notes which are to be so played. Some performers never employ the artificial mute, — a pear-shaped metal contrivance with perforations at the top, — but use the hand for both muted and stopped tones. It is, however, very difficult to mute the tones with the hand below and consequently the artificial mute must be used.

The effect of the mute is that of sounds coming from a distance or from a closed room. In *p*, *pp* or even *ppp* effects, or when an echo is desired, the mute is very reliable. If the mute is especially desired, rather than stopped tones, it should be indicated "con sordino" in the score, and "senza sordino" when required to be removed. The mute may be inserted before or during a phrase or passage.

The stopped tones of the horn are used when a veiled, dulled, depressed or muffled tone is desired, and may be varied in color from *p* to *ff*.

Examples

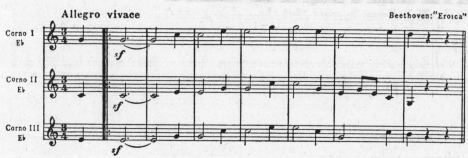

Allegro vivace   Beethoven: "Eroica"

Myerbeer: "Dinorah"

Tempo tranquillo   Henri Rabaud: "La Procession Nocturne"

Andante

Helen Dallam:"Indian Summer"

Poco lento

Paul Dukas:"Polyeucte"

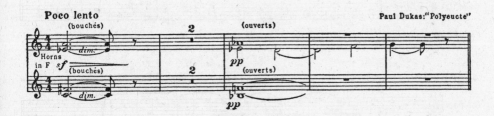

Fred. A. Stock:"C minor Symphony"

Piu animato

John A. Carpenter:"Perambulator Suite"

Allegro

Larghetto

Con sordini

John A. Carpenter:"Perambulator Suite"

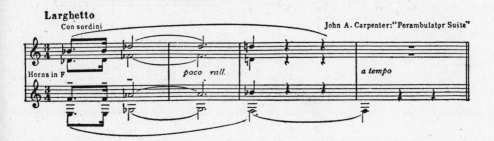

Mendelssohn's *Songs Without Words*

Exercise I. Arrange the first page of No. 3, *Hunting Song,* for three horns, strings and wood-winds.

Exercise II. Arrange the first twelve measures of No. 27 for four horns, strings and wood-winds.

Exercise III. Arrange a short hymn or choral for horns and wood-winds.

Exercise IV. Write a solo for horn with string accompaniment.

Exercise V. Arrange a baritone song for horn and strings.

Exercise VI. Arrange a male chorus for four horns.

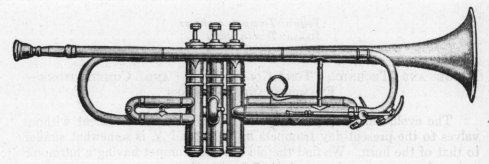

The Bb or A Trumpet

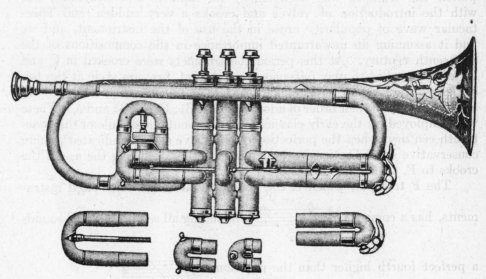

The Bb or A Cornet

CHAPTER XVII. THE VALVE TRUMPET

French: *Trompette a pistons*
Italian: *Tromba ventile*
German: *Ventiltrompete*

Range and Technic — Tone-Color, Uses and Combinations — Examples and Exercises

The evolution of the trumpet, from the earliest instrument without valves to the present-day trumpets in C, B♭ and A, is somewhat similar to that of the horn. We find the old natural trumpet having a harmonic series of

without intermediate tones of any real, dependable value. In this early period the trumpet was used chiefly for fanfares and flourishes, but with the introduction of valves and crooks a very sudden and spectacular wave of popularity arose in the use of the instrument, and we find it assuming an unwarranted importance in the compositions of the eighteenth century. At this period the trumpets were crooked in C and D, and were used to play passages of an elegant, bravura style at the top of the register. Later new crooks were added, until we find the following array of crooks in their order of adoption: E♭, B♭, F, E♮, B♮ and A. These were employed by the early classicists up to about the middle of the nineteenth century, when the perfection of the valve system indicated a more conservative specialization in the trumpet family, reducing the use of the crooks to F, C, B♭ and A.

The F trumpet, which is the last survival of the large-sized instruments, has a compass of ⟨musical notation⟩ including all semi-tones, and sounds

a perfect fourth higher than the notation: ⟨musical notation⟩

The upper part of the compass, from F to C ⟨musical notation⟩ is especially shrill and blatant, but in its lower register it is wonderfully strong and brilliant. The F trumpet, while still used in some of the foreign orchestras of to-day, has virtually given place to a smaller-sized instrument crooked in C, B♭ and A.

The C trumpet sounds as written.

The B♭ trumpet sounds a major second lower.

The A trumpet sounds a minor third lower.

In writing for the B♭ trumpet the signature should be that of the key a whole step higher.

In writing for the A trumpet the signature should be that of the key a minor third higher.

The same general observation as to which trumpet to use as was made for the B♭ and A clarinets holds good, — the A trumpet for sharp keys and the B♭ trumpet for flat keys.

These three crooks give the trumpets the following ranges:

We usually find that in symphonic compositions three trumpets are used, although in the works of the modernists we are not surprised to find four trumpet parts.

The most commonly employed trumpets are those crooked in B♭ and A, and the student is advised to score his trumpet parts for one or the other of these instruments. The C trumpet, which is still scored for in France and England, is gradually losing vogue in other countries.

The technic of the instrument, as well as its force of tone-color, prescribes for it definite uses in the orchestra ensemble. Its flourishes and fanfares are well known; but aside from these it does duty in all varieties of diatonic and arpeggic figuration, reiterations of tones, including double and triple tonguing on the same note, carrying the melody in tutti, especially in climaxes, and serving as the melody-carrying voice in the brass section.

In writing for two trumpets be sure to duet the parts, that is, to have them flow in thirds, sixths, augmented fourths and diminished fifths, just as one has learned to write in two-part counterpoint. Remember that the trumpets are predominating voices in the orchestra, and that a great deal of consideration should be given to their distinct and carrying tonal value. When the trumpet speaks in *f* or *ff*, it asserts itself in a very definite fashion, and should be tempered and balanced in so far as possible by the use of the horns and other brasses in order to give background for its vehemence. In *p* or *pp*, or in muted expression, it may assume a much more subdued importance, but it must be continually "watched and waited upon" by the composer, and surrounded by modifying orchestral friends.

The mute is used "con sordino, p" or "con sordino, f." In the latter of these two muted possibilities the tone is pungent and penetrating, and consequently must be used with consideration for its weird tonal picturization.

We must once again consider the ranges of these two instruments.

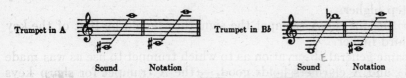

| Trumpet in A | | | Trumpet in B♭ | | |
| Sound | Notation | | Sound | Notation | |

As is the case with all wind instruments, the extremes of the registers are not the best parts in which to manifest striking and deliberate activities of expression, especially if that expression is sustained. To climax a melody in the high register is often necessary and effective, and to touch a note or two in the low register does not disturb the equilibrium of the performer; but to prolong either is more or less trying for the performer as well as for the listener.

The most gratifying range is between ⟨music⟩ regardless of the transposition.

The trill is performed only through the use of the valves, and, while not one of the instrument's most useful technical effects, it can be performed by some players with astonishing lightness and suavity. Grace notes give no trouble to the performer, nor do other simple varieties of ornamentation.

The student must be warned again about the performer's inability to breathe otherwise than normally, and in writing for the trumpet he must take this matter into consideration and phrase accordingly.

EXAMPLES

Mendelssohn's *Songs Without Words*

Exercise I. Arrange the first sixteen measures of No. 45 for trumpet and piano.

Exercise II. Arrange the first sixteen measures of No. 41 for woodwinds, horns, trumpet and strings.

Exercise III. Write a sixteen-measure fanfare for two trumpets.

Exercise IV. Compose a sketch in the large three-part form for two flutes, one oboe, two clarinets, bassoon, two horns, trumpet and strings.

THE BASS TRUMPET

French: *Trompette Basse*
Italian: *Tromba Bassa*
German: *Basstrompete*

While the bass trumpet finds very little use in the orchestra of to-day, it may occasionally be encountered in some of the important scores of the orchestral masters, and should be studied for score-reading purposes.

The bass trumpet is pitched in C, and is written for an octave higher than it sounds. Its compass is ⟨notation⟩ sounding ⟨notation⟩ The extreme register is almost impossible of performance and leaves a more or less flexible range of about two octaves: ⟨notation⟩ sounding one octave lower.

ILLUSTRATION

Bass trumpet in C

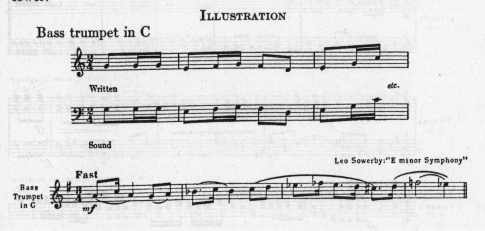

Leo Sowerby: "E minor Symphony"

THE CORNET

French: *Cornet-a-pistons*
Italian: *Cornetto*
German: *Cornett*

The cornet is a shorter and stubbier instrument than the trumpet, being lighter in tone-color and perhaps more flexible in execution.

It has the same range as the trumpet, and is crooked in C, B♭ and A. The B♭ and A are universally used in the smaller orchestras, and occasionally in the larger organizations for special effects.

All that was stated in regard to the technic, range of flexibility, ornamentation, tone-color, etc., for the trumpets holds good for the cornets. In fact, the cornet will perform more easily and more surely whatever is written for the trumpet than will the latter, but will not be as satisfactory in strength, volume and timbre.

The cornet is essentially a small orchestra brass, while the trumpet, being stronger in "tang," is essentially a large orchestra brass.

In the question of which instrument to choose for the various key signatures, use the B♭ cornet for the simple flat keys and the A cornet for the simple sharp keys. Where a number of sharps or flats are involved, it is well to consider enharmonic changes of keys, especially if the composition should happen to modulate into several extreme tonalities.

It is not often that orchestral compositions are written in the keys of G♭ major and C♭ major; but should such tonalities occur in a large composition in the way of modulations, the original key being D♭ major, the natural impulse will be to employ the B♭ cornet. This is carrying out the general rule that the B♭ crook be used for flat keys and the A crook for sharp keys. However, in considering enharmonic possibilities, we find that the A crook relieves the player of three accidentals.

Composition in D♭, the B♭ cornet plays in the key of 3 flats
Modulation into G♭, the B♭ cornet plays in the key of 4 flats
Modulation into C♭, the B♭ cornet plays in the key of 5 flats
_____
12 flats

Composition in D♭, enharmonically changed to C♯, the A cornet plays 4 sharps
Modulation into G♭, enharmonically changed to F♯, the A cornet plays 3 sharps
Modulation into C♭, enharmonically changed to B, the A cornet plays 2 sharps

———

9 sharps

The above deduction, while rather unusual, may find justification in any of the ultra-modern compositions, and the student will note that in writing for the transposing instruments he must consider the player as far as possible, in order to be rewarded thereby with a smoother, more graceful interpretation of his work. In orchestrating, no detail is too trivial for our attention, as study of the orchestral scores of the really great composers will demonstrate.

EXAMPLES

Grazioso con anima

Charles Wakefield Cadman: "I Hear a Thrush at Eve"

Cornet in B♭

Courtesy of the White-Smith Music Publishing Co.

Moderato

Charles Wakefield Cadman: "From the Land of the Sky-Blue Water"

Cornet in B♭

Courtesy of the White-Smith Music Publishing Co.

CHAPTER XVIII. THE TROMBONE

French: *Trombone*
Italian: *Trombone*
German: *Posaune*

RANGE, TECHNIC, PEDAL TONES AND COMBINATIONS WITH OTHER INSTRUMENTS — EXAMPLES — EXERCISES

The slide trombone, like the other brasses of the orchestra, has passed through a series of experimental stages. At the time of Bach four trombones were used. These were called soprano, or discant, alto, tenor and bass. In Wagner's day a double-bass trombone came into a short-lived vogue. These were all of the slide variety, and besides these, valve-trombones were invented, some of which are even now used in military bands.* Of these various high and low pitched instruments, the tenor trombone has survived and is the outstanding exponent of the trombone family.

It is non-transposing and has a range of two octaves and a diminished

fifth 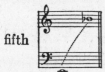 with all intermediate diatonic and chromatic tones. These

tones are all derived from a series of seven fundamentals and their harmonic overtones. The trombone with its slide closed tightly is pitched in B♭, and in this position the overtones of a dominant seventh chord with B♭ as the root are playable.

This is called the first position. By moving the slide downward a certain distance a new fundamental — a chromatic half step below — results. The further lengthening of the tubing produces still more fundamentals until the seven possible positions are exhausted. The composite result will be found as follows:

Natural or 1st Position | 2d Pos | 3d Pos. | 4th Pos. | 5th Pos. | 6th Pos. | 7th Pos.

---

* The valve-trombone is universally used in Italy, even in the orchestras.

The Trombone

Besides these tones there are three pedal tones of rather unsatisfactory timbre to be found an octave below the fundamentals of the first three positions.

Pedal Tones

The small notes indicated above the harmonic series are the ninth and tenth partials (including the pedal tones) which may be produced with a very strong lip. Ferdinand David, in his concertino for tenor trombone, employs these tones in several passages, but for general orchestral use they should be avoided. The three deep pedal tones are occasionally met with in scores, and should be approached either by a drop of an octave from the fundamental tone of the position being used, or following a pause. These tones require a very loose embouchure and should be used only in a sustained capacity and then in notes of not too long duration.

In the large symphony orchestras three trombones are employed, written on two bass clefs. The first and second occupy the first clef, and

the third shares the second clef with the tuba.

When the first and second trombone parts lie above the bass clef, necessitating the use of many leger lines, it is best to make use of the tenor clef to facilitate the reading.

Certain technical figures are awkward of performance on the trombone, necessitating, as they do, wide slides, such as from first to sixth positions, or second to seventh positions, or *vice versa*. These sudden and long sliding movements, especially in fast tempo, are often productive of ludicrous sounds and imperfect intonation, besides an unevenness of tone-production. The following progressions are some of the most difficult in

fast tempo:

Positions: 7

The foregoing progressions in medium or slow tempo, and even in moderately fast tempo when not repeated, such as [musical notation] are not difficult to perform. It is only when they are formed into a figure that they become difficult and unruly.

Trills, which are performed with the lips, are quite difficult of enunciation, and consequently are rarely found in orchestral music. The best register for their performance is between [musical notation]

The trombone is capable of a great variety of emotional expression: from sadness and brutality in its lowest register, strength, power, majesty and mildness in its middle and most flexible register, to tenderness, sharpness and brilliancy in its top register. Its principal uses in the orchestra ensemble are: the strengthening of the bass and tenor voices; harmonic background for the brasses; assistance in repeated notes of the trumpets and horns in lower voices of the quartet; its melody-singing possibilities in full orchestra against ornamentation in the strings and wood-winds; its vigorous and poignant expression in heroic climax; its mild, tender or sombre organ-like color in religious expression; and its wonderful rhythmic possibilities in martial music.

In writing for the trombone, avoid too many chromatics in succession unless you have made a very careful study of the slide positions and know what the performer has to cope with in the way of technic. Very fast work on the instrument is not satisfactory. Pure legato is not possible except when played on tones emanating from the same fundamental. If the slide is used, the time spent in the change up or down makes an unavoidable break, thus interrupting the flow. It is also well to remember that the trombonist plays by ear, and that if his ear is not perfectly pitched, involved melodies are very likely to be unsatisfactory. The trombone is an "impetus" instrument, requiring deliberate delineations of line, whether in straightforward melody or in sustained prolongation of tones, and should be treated as such, being allotted only those parts which are characteristic of its *raison d'être*.

THE BASS TROMBONE

The student will occasionally find parts scored for the bass trombone, a larger and deeper instrument than the B♭ tenor trombone, which has become the recognized instrument of the modern orchestra.

The two commonly played bass trombones are tuned in **G** and **F**, each with a range of two octaves and a diminished fifth. Their fundamentals are:

The G bass trombone is much easier to handle than the F trombone, which requires a more sturdy breath power than the former. Both instruments have pedal tones below their first three positions, which are rarely, if ever, used. Both of these trombones are non-transposing instruments, and are written for on the bass clef. As their use in the modern orchestra has been somewhat conservative of late years, — the three tenor trombones superseding the former two tenor and one bass trombone, — we shall mention only a few facts in regard to the instrument, but enough to enable the student to investigate should he desire a fuller knowledge of its possibilities.

All that has been said in regard to the technic of the tenor trombone, such as the avoidance of long slides in quick passage work, intricate melodies, trills, etc., should be even more strictly observed in considering the use of the bass trombone. Sustained tones in the lowest register are entirely a matter of lung power, and as the instrument is very hard to manipulate because of this reason, it should not be counted on to do extraordinary work of either a fast, or of a medium fast, staccato or broken chord nature. The instrument does not respond as quickly as does the tenor trombone, as the tubing is somewhat longer and a fraction of a second more is required for each slide movement. The best part of its range both in p and f expressions is:

EXAMPLES

Joyously

3 Trumpets

2 Trombones

3d Trombone & Tuba

Largo maestoso   B. Smetana:"Vyšehrad"

Trombones 1 2

Trombone 3 Tuba

Allegro vivace   Gustav Strube:"Symphony in B♭"

Trombones I II

Trombone III Tuba

Lento e lamentoso   Arne Oldberg:"Paolo E Francesca"

Trombones I II

Trombone III Tuba

Exercises. — The student should select suitable piano compositions for arrangement. He should make his selections with the special instrument in mind with which he is dealing. The trombones should not always be to the fore in the ensemble, but should be treated more as strong filling-in voices, doubling with the other deep voices of the orchestra and adding generally to the composite strength of the full tonal body. The trombones are used principally for full orchestral effects, for expressions of triumph, martial stimulation, rhythmic pulsations, and for underpinning in the brass choir.

Exercises.—The student should select suitable piano compositions for arrangement. He should make his selections with the special instrument in mind with which he is dealing. The trombones should not always be to the fore in the ensemble, but should be treated more as strong filling-in voices, doubling with the other deep voices of the orchestra, and adding generally to the composite strength of the full tonal body. The trombones are used principally for full orchestral effects, for expressions of triumph, martial stimulation, rhythmic pulsations, and for underpinning in the brass choir.

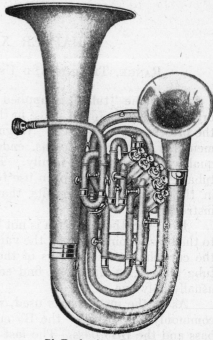

Bb Euphonium, Five-keyed

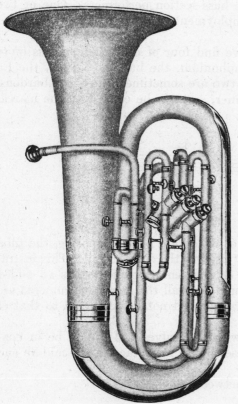

Eb Tuba

CHAPTER XIX. THE TUBA

Range, Technic and Uses — Examples — Exercises

The name "tuba" is applied to any of the several low bass valve-brasses that have found place in the orchestra from the earliest writers to the present-day composers. Wagner made use of a series of these instruments in his various operas, endeavoring to introduce a different tone quality into the brass family. These instruments are called "Wagner tubas," and, although not in use to-day, they were successfully employed in their time, giving results that cannot be duplicated on any other instruments.

However, the orchestra is not lacking in the deep bass tones necessary to the brass choir, although the variety of blends has been reduced through the curtailment in numbers of the bass-section performers. One or two tuba players, at the most, find employment in our modern orchestra — usually only one.

As to the instruments used, we find four of different compass quite commonly employed, — the B♭ euphonium, the bass tuba in F, the E♭ bass and the BB♭ bass. The last two are sometimes called bombardons, and when curled in a circular manner, so as to be carried on the march, receive the name of helicons.

| Euphonium | Tuba in F | E♭ bass | BB♭ bass |
| B♭ four valves | four valves | four valves | three valves |

Of these four instruments, all of which are non-transposing, the tuba in F is perhaps the most commonly used in the concert hall. This instrument when fitted with the fourth or compensating piston has an added range similar to that of the BB♭ tuba. As all the newer instruments are fitted with this fourth valve, the range need not be restricted to that of the three-valved tuba.

Trills on the tuba are made with the valves and should be in conjunction with a single valve. These should find place in the middle and

upper registers of the instrument between

153

If used for orchestral purposes, the trill should be doubled in another brass in order to soften to some degree the roughness of the effect. By itself the tuba is "blurty," preponderating and overbearing, especially in *f* or *ff*. It should always be played in company with other brasses or in full orchestra, and even then with due consideration for its powerful, far-reaching tone qualities. In *pp*, *p* or *mp*, the tone is more satisfactory and mixes well with its brass relatives. Its uses are not so numerous as are those of the trombone, but in its few duties it is a much-needed adjunct to the orchestra.

Doubling in the lower octave with the third trombone is one of its most common uses, just as one finds the double-bass doubling with the cello.

Playing bass melody with other bass instruments, or occasionally bass counter-melodies of its own, especially in *p* and legato.

Acting as pedal to the brass choir is another of its functions.

Adding volume in brass tutti, or full orchestra where a boisterous climax is desired, finds the tuba in its natural element.

In marking the rhythm, as does the double-bass, it is effective and stimulating if not overdone.

Taking part in the general harmonization, where, in tonal coloring, it reminds one of the deep stops of the organ, is one of its most characteristic features of performance.

The student will do well not to demand extremely difficult technical feats of the tuba player; for while the capable players exhibit ease and facility in execution, the instrument itself, being large and cumbersome, is difficult to play, requiring much more lung power than any other brass, and consequently taxing the player to the utmost.

The music for the tuba shares the bass clef with the third trombone, or is given a separate clef to itself. The signature of the composition is used.

The pedal tones are weak and practically useless, although sometimes employed. They are performed with a loose lip and are liable to be faulty in intonation. The student is advised against their use to any great extent.

The Bb Euphonium
Four-keyed

The Double Bb Tuba

EXAMPLES

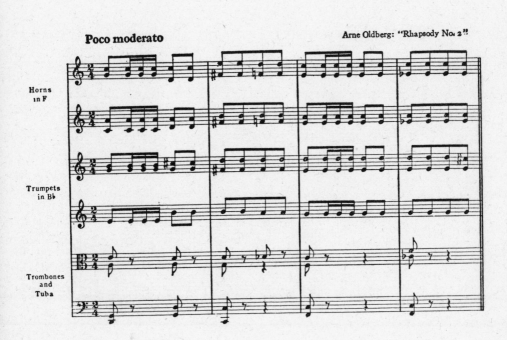

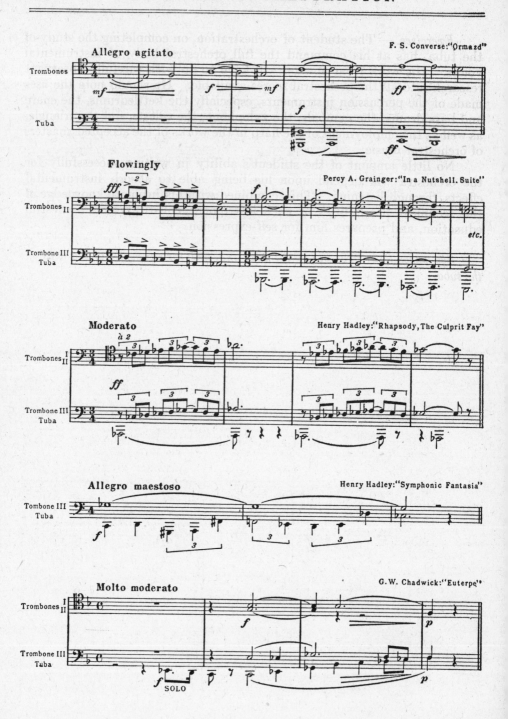

Exercises. — The student of orchestration, on completing the study of the tuba, has at his command the full orchestral body of instrumental voices. His work from now on will have to do with carefully observant research into all the orchestral scores available. He should note the uses made of the percussion instruments, especially the kettledrums, the snare and bass drums, the cymbals, the xylophone, the celesta and the triangle, as well as the employment of the harp in the works of the accepted masters of orchestral music.

No little amount of the student's ability in writing successfully for the orchestra will depend upon his being able to absorb instrumental effects through listening. This, combined with his intimate knowledge of the technical possibilities of each instrument, constitutes his orchestral education, and prepares him for self-expression.

See pages 214, 215, 217, 220, 222, 223, 231 for examples of the uses of the tuba.

CHAPTER XX. THE SAXOPHONES

Italian: *Sassophone*
French: *Saxophone*
German: *Saxophon*

The instruments of the saxophone family, which are very rarely used in symphonic music, and which are at present used mainly in military bands and "jazz" orchestras, partake partly of the quality of the wood-winds and partly of that of the brass, though they are generally classed with the wood-winds, as their technique, and, to some extent, their tone quality, is much like that of certain of the wood-wind instruments.

There are many different saxophones, and though they are all trans-posing, they are all written for in identical fashion. The most commonly used saxophones are the soprano in B♭, alto in E♭, tenor in B♭ and baritone in E♭.

The written range for all the saxophones is

The notes given at the top of the range in quarter notes are rather difficult to produce.

The soprano saxophones do not possess the high F.

Many of the older saxophones do not possess the low B♭.

The soprano saxophone in B♭, like the B♭ clarinet, is written one whole tone higher than the actual pitch. Its sounding range is therefore:

(as it lacks the top F, as shown above).

The alto saxophone in E♭ is written a major sixth higher than the actual pitch. Its sounding range is as follows:

The tenor saxophone in B♭, like the bass clarinet in B♭, is written a major ninth higher than the actual pitch. Its sounding range is:

C Melody Tenor

Bb Bass

Eb Soprano

Eb Alto

Eb Baritone

Bb Tenor

Bb Soprano

The Saxophone Family

The baritone saxophone in E♭ is written an octave and a major sixth higher than the actual pitch.   Its sounding range is:

It must be borne in mind that all the saxophones are always written for in the treble clef.

The E♭ soprano saxophone, a small instrument with a rather piercing tone quality, is occasionally used in "jazz" orchestras.   It has the range of the B♭ soprano saxophone, but is written for as is the E♭ clarinet, a minor third below the actual pitch.

The so-called C-melody saxophone is a tenor saxophone sounding one octave below the written notes.   It is gradually going out of use, and is never written for in military bands or in orchestras.   It has always been more or less an amateur's instrument.

The tone quality of the saxophones is mellow and full, sonorous and fairly penetrating.   The saxophones are perhaps best used as solo instruments; though when several saxophones are used in a group, the effect is unlike any other which can be produced in the orchestra for richness and mellowness.   The most legitimate use of the saxophones is in legato passages, though a remarkably crackling effect can be produced by the use of several saxophones playing chord staccato.

When used with other instruments the characteristic tone quality of the saxophone tends to be obscured, though the use of one or two saxophones doubling strings, wood-winds or horns in the tenor, or even in other registers, puts a remarkable "edge" on a melodic passage, and results in an unusually sonorous effect.

With the "slap-tongue," "glissando" and other effects exploited by saxophonists in "jazz" orchestras, this treatise is not particularly concerned, and the student is advised to study them at close range by actually hearing them, for only in this way can they be thoroughly understood.

THE SARRUSOPHONE

French: *Sarrusophone*
Italian: *Sarrusofone*
German: *Sarrusophon*

The sarrusophone, a metal instrument closely related to the bassoon, is made in six sizes:

Soprano in B♭.	Baritone in E♭.
Alto in E♭.	Bass in B♭.
Tenor in B♭.	Contrabass in E♭.

These instruments are all notated for on the treble clef, and each has the same written range: Being transposing instruments they sound as follows:

The bass in B♭ and contrabass in E♭ have a very low range, infringing on the ranges of the bassoon and contrabassoon, for which instruments they occasionally substitute. French writers, apparently, are acquiring a taste for the sarrusophone in orchestral works, but we believe that the instrument finds its normal and natural habitat in the brass band family.

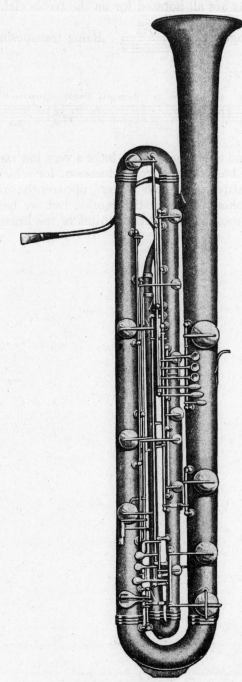

The Sarrusophone

The Double-Action Harp

CHAPTER XXI. THE HARP

French: *La Harpe*
Italian: *Arpa*
German: *Harfe*

The harp is at present a diatonic instrument of forty-seven strings

tuned in the key of C♭ major. Its compass is from low C♭

to

Its music is written on two clefs, as for the piano, the bass and treble clefs being employed. There are seven transposing pedals, D♭ C♭ B♭ to the left, and E♭ F♭ G♭ A♭ to the right. Between these pedals is an extra pedal used for dynamic purposes and called the forte pedal.

Each pedal may be depressed two notches by the foot, thus raising the tones one-half step above their pitch when placed in the first notch, and one whole step when in the second. Thus, if the B♭ pedal is depressed, all B♭ strings become B; if depressed into the second notch, B♯ results throughout the entire compass of the harp on the B♭ strings. Thus it will be seen that the pedals must be "set" for each tonality required, and that involved chromatic passages are impossible of performance.

THE HARP PEDALS

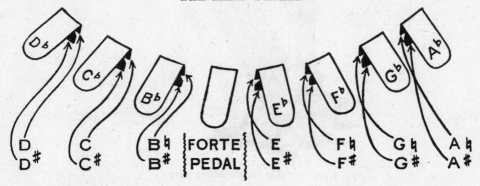

In considering the illustration of the harp pedals the student will observe that enharmonic notes are not difficult to obtain in certain instances.

161

By depressing the B♭ pedal one notch we find it enharmonic with C♭: B — C♭.

By depressing the E♭ pedal to the second notch we get E♯ enharmonic with its neighboring string F: E♯ — F.

In this same manner of pedaling the strings, further enharmonic pairs of tones will result, such as: D♭ — C♯, D♯ — E♭, E — F♭, F♯ — G♭, G♯ — A♭, A♯ — B♭, and B♯ — C.

As the single harp string is not adapted for the performance of repeated notes, the enharmonic unisons above indicated permit of this tonal repetition of the nine tones made possible through pedaling.

Glissando passages covering six octaves are possible and effective, though such technical effects should not be overdone. They are usually

indicated  but may be partially written in and con-

nected: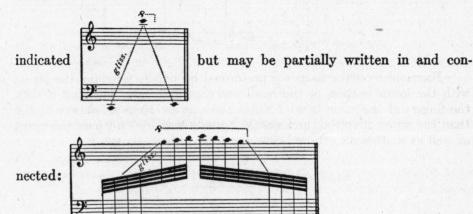

Intervals of thirds and sixths are playable if not chromatic.

Fast or slow

The same is true of sixths.

Modulations to distant keys that necessitate the notching of more than two pedals are quite difficult, especially if required to be performed rapidly. Modulations which require but one pedal change are not difficult.

Tremolos are not difficult, nor are trills if written for adjacent tones. Neither is especially effective.

Through the enharmonic double-toning of the harp strings various chords of the seventh result, and may be effectively employed either as arpeggios, glissandos, chords or tremolos.

Harmonics on the harp are performed by lightly touching the string with the lower portion of the hand and simultaneously plucking it with the fingers of the same hand. This causes an overtone an octave higher than the string involved, and should be indicated by "o" over the notes as well as written an octave below the tone desired, thus:

Harmonics should be employed only where a rather deliberate melody is desired in *p* or *pp*, and either with a very soft accompaniment of another harp or a similar pizzicato accompaniment in the strings. The harmonics are easily "lost" if too much is going on in the orchestra. They are best

in the middle and upper registers, between

Two or three harmonics may be played at once by the left hand but only one by the right hand; this makes chords of harmonics possible, though only effective when everything else is reduced, dynamically, to a minimum.

Stopped tones, called "sons étouffés," are effected by stopping the string-vibrations immediately after plucking, thus deadening the tones and giving the effect of dull pizzicato in the strings. This is indicated "stopped," and "let vibrate" when no longer desired. The French terms are "sons étouffés" and "laissez vibrer."

"Sons pres de la table" (sounds near the sounding board), which give a queer, somewhat metallic quality of sound, result from plucking the strings with the finger nails as close to the sounding board as possible. These are called "sons d'onglas" (guitar sounds), and should be indicated "guitar sounds" or "sons pres de la table," and a dotted line carried to the point where they should stop.

In scoring for the harp a few pertinent observations should be carefully considered by the student.

1. Harp music, in order to be effective, should be scored in a manner to be easily and naturally playable. The harpist uses but four fingers of each hand, the little finger remaining idle. The strings of the harp, being considerably closer together than the keys of the piano, permit of a chord stretch of at least a tenth, rather than the conventional octave of the piano. The harpist, then, plays four notes with each hand, either simultaneously or in arpeggic formation, but he should not be called on to play notes that have just been plucked by the opposite hand. In other words, do not overlap the tones of one hand into those of the other. As most of the music written for the harp will be of the arpeggic variety, the student should give these remarks serious attention. Furthermore, the two hands should not be required to perform arpeggios in the two extremes of the register at the same time, as the effect will be most unsatisfactory. The nearer the arpeggios are "bunched" in the middle register, the better will be the resultant effects. If the arpeggios are up and down the entire register of the instrument, they should be written in one voice or part, each hand performing not over four notes of the arpeggic stream.

2. Occasionally two harps are indicated in the scoring of an involved composition. This does not necessarily mean that they should be played in unison, although this is sometimes the case where added harp volume is desired. It does, however, offer an opportunity for the composer to divide the chromatic passages between the two instruments, permitting a more successful rendition of involved figures than one harp alone could possibly receive. To do this requires considerable study of the music to be performed in relation to the pedal possibilities of the instrument.

3. Enharmonically changing sharp keys to flats, such as B to C♭, F♯ to G♭, etc., is a most desirable practice, and should always be effected, even if only for a short part of a composition, providing strings do not have to be notched differently too quickly; not, however, for a few measures.

4. Four-part harmony, three notes in one hand and octaves in the other in the form of an accompaniment, often finds place.

Rolled chords are commonly employed.

For other varieties of technic the student should make a close study of Parish Alvars' *Concerto* for harp, Reinecke's *Concerto* for harp, and Schücker's Op. 11 and Op. 12. These, with a close observation of all the harp parts in whatever scores he can make available, will enable him to write fluently and correctly for the instrument.

In 1894, a chromatic harp was patented in Paris by the firm of Pleyel & Cie. This instrument was further perfected in 1904 by M. Gustave Lyon, the chief director of the firm, and it is now on the market. The instrument has no pedals, and the strings are arranged in a crisscross pattern, so that those representing the white keys of the piano find place on the left side of the console and the right side of the sound-board, while those representing the black keys of the piano are attached to the right side of the console and the left side of the sound-board.

The tuning arrangement is somewhat different from that of the diatonic harp, the new ingenious details greatly facilitating this arduous labor in an instrument of so many strings. The range is the same as that of the ordinary harp.

The chromatic harp seems to be the subject of great contention in the harp players' world, some favoring its use while others are bitterly opposed to it. Those who favor its use claim that it offers unlimited possibilities to the composer, who, in writing for the diatonic harp, must confine his expression to more or less diatonic musical invention, thus cramping his utterance to fit the shortcomings of the instrument.

The diatonic harp performer claims that it is impossible to keep the newer instrument in tune; that the tonal results are consequently unsatisfactory; that the technic is awkward, ungainly and unnatural to the hands; and finally, that even though the composer is somewhat hampered in his expression in writing for the older instrument, the results are artistically more satisfying. Be all this as it may, the chromatic harp is gaining in popularity in the European orchestras, and it has been adopted over the older instrument by the Brussels Conservatory of Music.

EXERCISES

C. A. Debussy: "La Mer"

Moderement anime

First
Harp

Second
Harp

Harmonics

Vincent d'Indy: "B♭ Major Symphony"

Extrêmement lent.

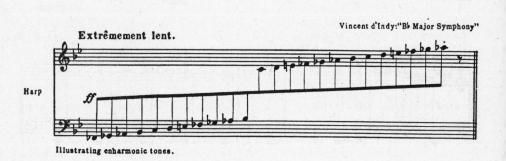

Harp

Illustrating enharmonic tones.

Presto   Granville Bantock: "Pierrot of the Minute"

Harp

Staccato notes.

Moderato

Clar. Bb

Leo Sowerby: "Harp Concerto"

Harp

A difficult bit involving pedal shifts.

etc.

F. Delius: "Brigg Fair"

Moderato

Octave passages.

C.A. Debussy:"La Mer"

Moderement anime

Leo Sowerby:"Comes Autumn Time"

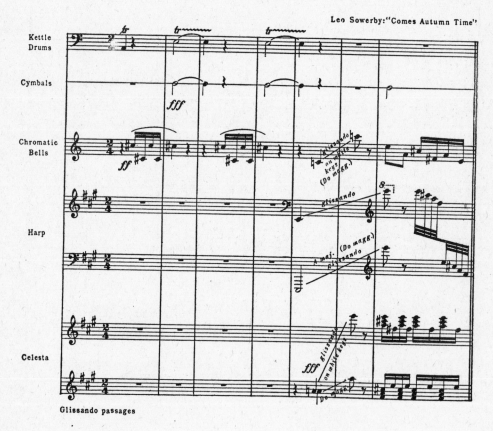

Glissando passages

Old Style-Kettledrums

CHAPTER XXII. THE PERCUSSION INSTRUMENTS

Those instruments which are set into vibration through being struck, either with a specially designed hammer, stick or piece of metal or through coming into contact with their like, or with the hand, are called percussion instruments. Of these instruments but five are capable of producing sounds of definite and intended pitch, the others giving off a rhythmical, accelerating noise.

Tuned Percussions	*Untuned Percussions*
1. Kettledrums.	1. Snare drum.
2. Bells (Tubular).	2. Bass drum.
3. Orchestra bells.	3. Tambourine.
4. Celesta.	4. Triangle.
5. Xylophone and marimba.	5. Cymbals.
	6. The gong or tam-tam.
	7. Castanets.

In the small orchestra of to-day, these instruments come under the general appellation of "traps," and very often one performer will have as many as eight or more different varieties carefully distributed about him in a convenient arrangement, easy to the hand, and will do his duty by all of them in a surprisingly agile and clever manner. Such a performer is called a "traps player." He must be a person of vivid imagination and good rhythmical discrimination, for he rarely uses music by which to be guided, depending entirely on his genius for improvisation to carry him along. Results are not always satisfactory, but nevertheless a rhythmical stimulation, sometimes bordering on hysteria, results; and as that seems to be his main object in life, he appears to fulfill his mission in a magnificent and grandiose fashion.

In considering the percussions we will not take the gentleman of the "traps" into our scheme of arrangement, for he belongs to the small dance or moving-picture orchestra. In the larger orchestras each percussion instrument has its individual performer except in the matter of triangle or castanets, where one player may "double" in the parts, provided he is not too busily occupied with his own specialty.

Music for the percussions is written above the strings (including the harp) and below the brasses. This will be further detailed as each instrument is taken up and explained.

169

TUNED PERCUSSIONS

The Kettledrums

French: *Timbales*
Italian *Timpani*
German: *Pauken*

We now come to the tuned percussions, all of which are important factors in the modern orchestra. The kettledrums, which were formerly rhythmical accentuators, have developed into definite melodic, as well as rhythmic, instruments. This elevation, which found its first demonstration in the works of Beethoven, has brought the kettledrums into such prominence as to necessitate a performer of keen musical and discriminating artistry.

Up to the days of Beethoven, but two kettledrums were used in the concert orchestra. These were tuned tonic and dominant. With the introduction of a third kettledrum, various tunings began to appear; but the roots of the three fundamental triads — tonic, dominant and subdominant — were the three tones usually employed. The kettledrums may be re-tuned to agree with a change of tonality during the course of a composition, but the performer must be allowed ample time in which to make the required changes. He should never be expected to make rapid changes of any sort, but should be given sufficient time to adjust and test the drumheads. This he does by tightening or loosening the parchment by means of several tuning handles distributed around the drumhead.

The three drums commonly employed in the large orchestras are called small, middle and large drums. Their range is:

If the bowl of the third drum is large enough, the two lowest tones in brackets are procurable and are often called for in compositions. The composer should indicate the tunings of his drums at the beginning of the kettledrum part:

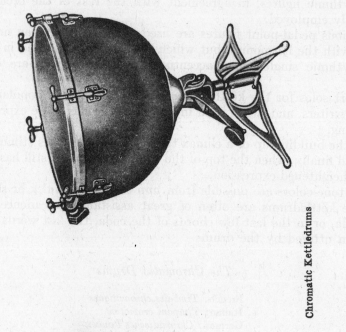

Chromatic Kettledrums

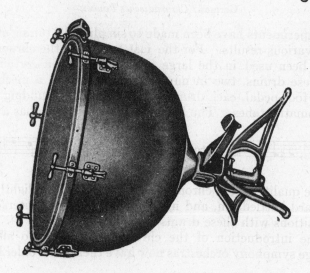

In writing the kettledrum part be sure to indicate clearly and concisely the exact expression expected.   This is very important, as the drummer cannot be expected to guess the composer's intentions and so cannot be blamed if he plays *ff* where *pp* is desired.

Short or long rolls are characteristic and effective.

Rhythmic figures, in agreement with the rest of the orchestra, are commonly employed.

Various pedal-point figures are used which may or may not be consonant with the harmonics, but which should begin and end in harmony.

Rhythmic single-stroke accentuations or pulsations are commonly used.

Short solos for the kettledrums have become quite popular with the modern writers, and, when used in their proper places, are expressive and interesting.

In the building up of a climax the kettledrum creates stimulation and urge, and finally, when the top of the climax is reached, still has power for further heightened expression.

All tone-colors are possible from *ppp* to *fff* with quick or slow tempi.

The kettledrums are often of great assistance in cadences.   In the final coda, or in the last few chords of the coda, the last words in finality are often uttered by the drums.

The Chromatic Drums

French: *Timbales chromatiques*
Italian: *Timpani cromatici*
German: *Chromatischer Pauken*

Many experiments have been made to simplify the tuning of the kettledrums with various results.   For the last few years the chromatic kettledrums have been used in the large orchestras with a certain degree of success.   These drums, two in number, are tuned by a mechanism controlled by a foot-pedal, each drum being capable of sounding four whole, or eight chromatic, tones.   The larger of the two drums has a range from

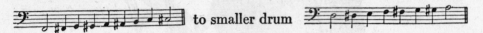
to smaller drum

The tone quality of the chromatic drums varies but slightly from that of the standard kettledrum, and many of the modern writers are scoring their compositions with these drums in mind.

With the introduction of the chromatic drums into all orchestras (only the large symphony orchestras now have them), the older kettledrums will gradually disappear, except, perhaps, one retained for special uses, such as certain low tunings; but even this old drum will eventually be superseded by the further introduction of an extra low-pitched mechanical drum.

EXAMPLES

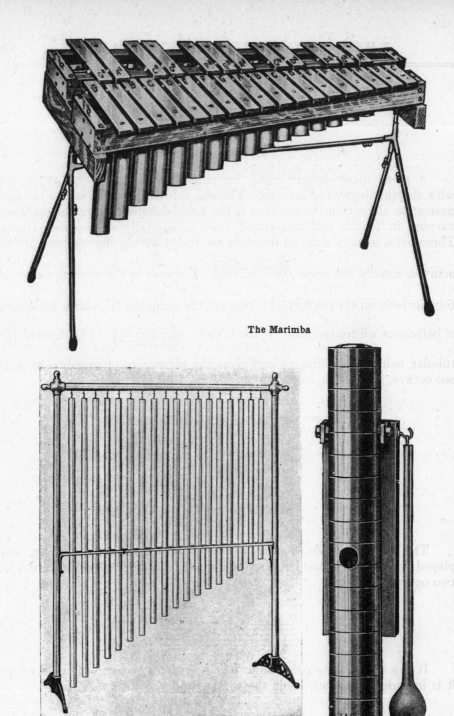

The Marimba

Cathedral Chimes

The Cathedral Chimes

French: *Cloches*
Italian: *Campane*
German: *Glocken*

A great many substitutions for church bells have been attempted with varying degrees of success. The one substitute which seems to come nearest to answering the purpose is the tubular bells, a set of metal tubes varying in length and suspended from a specially constructed frame. These bells, usually eight in number, are tuned within the compass of two

octaves, usually between  Because of the various makes of

tubular bells on the market, it is best for the composer to confine his sphere

of bell-tones within the limits of the G clef:  The tone of the

tubular bell is very illusive and gives the impression of sounding at least one octave, if not two, lower than it is actually pitched.

Orchestra Bells

French: *Carillon*
Italian: *Campanelli*
German: *Glockenspiel*

The orchestra bells, a series of steel plates tuned in chromatics and played with wooden, hard rubber or hard felt hammers, has a compass of two octaves or more.

It is a transposing percussion, being written two octaves below where it is intended to sound; thus the written range will be

It is bright and crystal-clear in tone-color, and is used principally to brighten a melody or to heighten an effect in the upper registers of the strings and wood-winds. In scoring for the orchestra bells, a great variety of technic is possible, as the instrument is almost purely melodic rather than harmonic, although double notes may occasionally be inserted in the part.

EXAMPLES

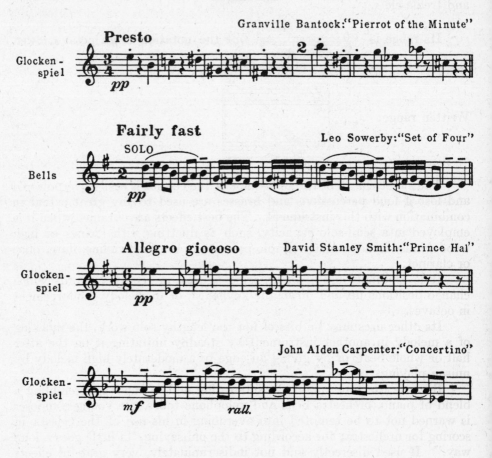

The Celesta

The celesta is also a series of steel plates under each of which is a wooden resonator, which gives to the instrument a very beautiful tone quality. These steel plates and resonators are mounted in a case to which is added a simple piano keyboard and a damper pedal. It is, therefore, played in the same manner as the piano, and the music is written on the bass and treble clefs.

Its range is 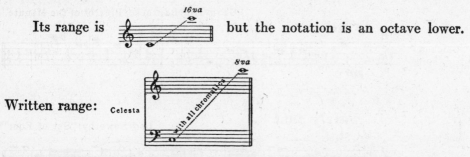 but the notation is an octave lower.

Written range:

The sweet charm of the tone-color of the celesta is easily overpowered and lost if loud percussions and brasses are used to any great extent in combination with this instrument. The best effects are obtained when it is employed in a semi-solo capacity, such as duetting with strings or high wood-winds, or accompanying solo passages in the first violins, flute, oboe or clarinet.

It is especially useful in arpeggio figures, in repeated chords which change positions up and down the keyboard, or in melody reinforcement in octaves.

Its other uses may be bits of not too lengthy solo work, the mocking of a melody in another instrument by steadily imitating it on the after half or whole beat, or by giving an edge to a moderately high melody by unison playing.

Because the tone quality is interesting and attractive, resembling a blend of piano, orchestra bells and xylophone tones, the young composer is warned not to be tempted into overdoing in his use of the celesta in scoring for orchestra; for according to the old saying, "a little goes a long way." If used discreetly and not indiscriminately, very grateful effects may be obtained, and in this instance it is better underdone than overdone.

EXAMPLES

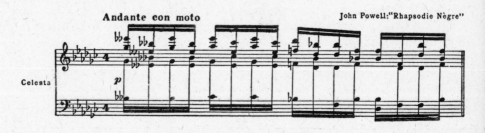

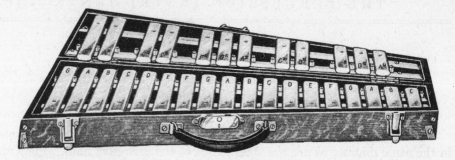

Orchestra Bells

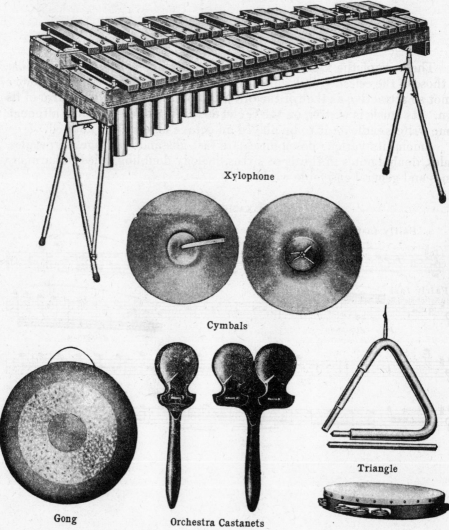

Xylophone

Cymbals

Gong

Orchestra Castanets

Triangle

Tambourine

The Xylophone

French: *Xylophone*
Italian: *Silofono*
German: *Xylophon*

The xylophone consists of a series of wooden plates or bars arranged in the same manner as are the steel plates of the orchestra bells. They are played upon with wooden, hard rubber or hard felt hammers (or beaters) and have a combined range of three octaves with all chromatics:

The bars of the xylophone are fitted with wooden resonators similar to those of the celesta; and while the quality of the sound of the xylophone is not so attractive as that of the celesta, it still has a peculiar charm of its own. Its music is written on the G clef as it is intended to sound, although some writers indicate it to be played an octave higher than notated.

Among its various possibilities are fast glissando passages, arpeggios, scales, double notes in thirds or sixths, melody doubling, filled-in harmony tones and general ensemble work.

EXAMPLES

The Marimba

The marimba, or, as it is sometimes called, marimbaphone, belongs to the same family as the xylophone and orchestra bells. The bars of the marimba are made of hard wood, and vary in width from one and five-eighths to two and one-fourth inches. The chromatic range is four octaves, C to C,* and the tone quality is strikingly mellow and somewhat similar to the pipe organ in depth and color.

Each bar is equipped with a resonating tube which individualizes and helps to sustain the vibrations, thus making the instrument particularly suitable for melodies of a somewhat slower tempo than would seem appropriate for either the xylophone or bells.

The performer uses two mallets; and as there are several varieties to choose from, gradating from tightly wound to loosely wound heads, he uses those which he thinks are most appropriate for the music being performed.

It is only of late years that the marimba has found place in the serious orchestras of the country, its use being strikingly illustrated in *The Warriors*, and the suite, *In a Nutshell*, by Percy A. Grainger.

Percy A. Grainger: "In a Nutshell Suite"

THE UNTUNED PERCUSSIONS

The Snare Drum

French: *Tambour* or *Caisse claire*
Italian: *Tamburo militare*
German: *Kleine Trommel*

The snare drum, side drum or military drum is a cylinder-shaped metal instrument covered at both ends by tightly stretched sheepskin. This is the smallest of the drums, and is beaten, or played, with two wooden drumsticks. Across the lower parchment are the tightly stretched snares, one, two, three or four in number, which resemble the catgut strings of the violin. These snares vibrate in exact sympathy with stick strokes on the batter-head, thus creating a decidedly poignant sound. By loosening the snares the quality of the tone becomes less poignant, and by inserting a

---

* Different manufacturers of tuned percussions make instruments varying in range; and since the ranges are not entirely standardized, the composer should indicate at the beginning of his score the range he wishes to use.

handkerchief or bit of cloth between the snares and the snarehead the tone becomes muffled.

The snare drum is purely a rhythmical instrument, and, as a consequence, performs all rhythmic combinations with ease.   One of its most

characteristic duties is the roll:

This can be performed in any shading from *pp* to *ff* or

In scoring for the snare drum the exact rhythmical motives of the music are generally employed, although, on occasion, a syncopated drum figure is used to heighten and brighten an effect requiring extra snap and vigor.

In military music, the drum plays a conspicuous part, and often, for long periods at a time, the drums will relieve the rest of the band by playing various march combinations, such as:

For average marching.

For rather slow plodding or for funeral marching

For a brisk, double-quick gait.

The bass drum is used on the strong accents of measures, sometimes on the strong and weak accents, as will be noted above.

There are so many figures possible on the drum that it would be useless to enumerate them; but the student should study the few appended examples, which will aid him in his work.   The drum is notated on the treble clef, or on a single line, and the same is true of all the untuned percussions which, in the orchestral score, find place above the kettledrum staff.

EXAMPLES

Andantino quasi allegretto

EXAMPLES

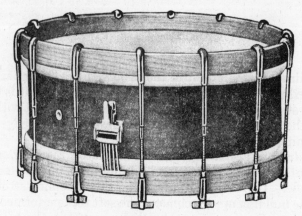

Snare Drum

Bass Drum   Bass Drum Stick

The Bass Drum

French: *Grosse Caisse*
Italian: *Gran Cassa*
German: *Grosse Trommel*

The bass drum is the largest of the drums, the cylinder barrel of which is wood, covered at both ends with tightened parchment. It is beaten with a felt-knobbed stick, which, when coming into sharp contact with the drumhead, creates the slow vibrations of the low bass drum language with which we are all so familiar.

The bass drum is also a rhythmical stimulator, marking, as it usually does, the accents in martial music and adding urge and excitement to the general ensemble. Its few other uses include the booming strokes so often employed in the building up of a climax; the soft roll, performed with either one or two drumsticks, or with two kettledrum sticks; the occasional soft, single stroke introduced into a composition to express fear or mystery. The bass drum may be muffled by loosening the heads or by covering them with a cloth. The muffled drums are used for funeral marches or compositions depicting sorrow or death.

The bass drum is notated on the bass clef or on a single line, thus:

The bass drum sometimes shares one staff with another percussion in the conductor's score, but should be written on separate staffs for the player's part.

In some orchestras, the bass drummer is often required to play the cymbals as well as the bass drum. This is managed through firmly attaching one of the cymbal plates to the top of the drum-barrel and striking it with the other plate which is held in the left hand by means of the strap. This permits the freedom of the right hand for bass drum service.

Another method of simultaneously employing both of these instruments is by means of a mechanical device consisting of levers and a pedal manipulated by foot-power, which allows the performer the freedom of both hands for other duties. Such a performer is called traps-player.

While the simultaneous performance of several percussion instruments by one player may serve the purpose in small orchestras, it is never satisfactory in the large orchestra, where decided individuality of tonal expression is demanded. Here each instrument should be played by an individual performer.

EXAMPLES

For other examples of drum technic, see pages 220, 221, 222, 223, 227, 235.

The Tambourine

French: *Tambourine*
Italian: *Tamburino*
German: *Tambourin*

The tambourine, which belongs to the drum family, consists of a wooden or metal hoop, on one side of which is stretched a vellum head, the other side being open. Five or six pairs of small thin metal plates, called jingles, are set loosely on wires in slots made around the hoop, so that when the instrument is shaken, or struck by the knuckles on the vellum head, these metal discs respond or jingle. Another effect is produced by rubbing the vellum with the thumb, creating a trill and jingle combined.

The instrument is more especially native to the music of Spain than to any other country, although very appropriate to Oriental musical expression in compositions in the dance idiom.

In notating for this instrument, use either the staff or a single line, indicating the exact rhythm to be employed:

In ballet music, the tambourine is often played by the dancers, and in some ballet schools the instrument receives special attention in the curriculum.

It is at present used quite frequently in both large and small orchestras, any percussion player being capable of performing upon this instrument.

Weber was one of the first composers to incorporate the tambourine into the orchestra in an artistic manner. See his overture to *Preciosa*.

Examples

The Triangle

French: *Triangle*
Italian: *Triangolo*
German: *Triangel*

This instrument is a steel bar a quarter of an inch or more in thickness, bent into the shape of a triangle the ends of which are not joined. It is played by striking it with a thin bar of the same metal, giving forth a clear, penetrating tone of somewhat indistinct intonation. The music for the triangle is written on the treble clef and should comprise only an occasional rhythmic touch, or a slight roll at the end of a crescendo. It is an extraordinarily assertive little instrument capable of being heard in *ff* over an orchestral *ff* tutti. By contrast it is charming in reticence when played very softly with the strings and wood-winds *pp* in their high registers. It is used a great deal in ballet music, less frequently in light opera, occasionally in grand opera, and but rarely in serious orchestral music. When using it for the concert orchestra the student will do well first to make a thorough investigation of its traditions in this respect. Among other things he will discover that it is used, when employed at all, only for one or two "touches" in an entire score, or for a short roll in a climax.

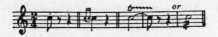

The triangle may also be written on a single line in the same manner as the tambourine part.

EXAMPLES

Vincent d'Indy:"2d Symphony"

The foregoing example is taken from the third movement of Vincent d'Indy's *Second Symphony*, and is used with full or rather full orchestra.

See pages 219, 227, 235, for examples of the various uses of the triangle.

Allegro grazioso

F. S. Converse:"Festival of Pan"

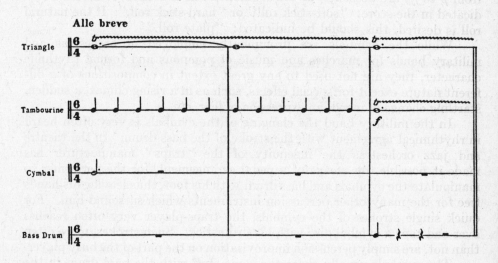

The Cymbals

French: *Cymbales*
Italian: *Piatti*
German: *Becken*

We are all familiar with the two large thin brass plates, held one in each hand by a strap, which are clanged together, producing an almost ear-splitting crash.

The cymbals are not always used for the purpose of making a banging noise, although in the military bands or in comic opera they usually serve this purpose. They are capable of a light touch here and there or of a roll produced by suspending one of the plates and beating it with two snare drumsticks or two kettledrum sticks. Another manner of roll is produced by setting the plates in vibration by a circular, brushing movement, the hands moving in opposite directions. In the rolls, varying degrees of sound from *p* to *fff* are possible. If the drumstick-roll is desired, it should be indicated in the score: "soft-stick roll" or "hard-stick roll." If the natural roll is desired, this should be indicated: "plate roll."

While the cymbals are prominently employed in orchestras and military bands for marches and music of pompous and formal rhythmic character, they are not used to any great extent in compositions of a different nature except for special effects, such as in a rising climax, a sudden, startling change of mood, an expression of fear, etc.

In the military band the clanging of the cymbals is very often heard in rhythmical agreement with the stroke of the bass drum. In the theatre and jazz orchestras the ingenuity of the "traps" manufacturer has made it possible, by means of a pedal arrangement, for the performer to manipulate the cymbals and bass drum with his foot, thus leaving his hands free for the many other percussion instruments which surround him. For quick single strokes of the cymbals, the traps-player very often reaches over and taps a cymbal disc with his drumstick. Such strokes, more often than not, are simply percussion improvisation on the part of the busy player.

The cymbals usually share the same staff with the bass drum in the score, but should be notated separately for the performer.

EXAMPLES

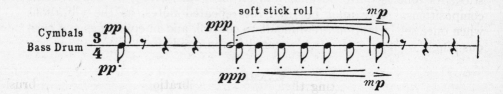

Leo Sowerby: "Set of Four"

Cymbal hung up and played
with wooden sticks.

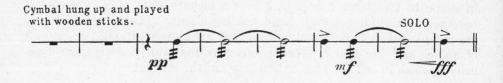

The Gong, or Tam-Tam

The gong, or tam-tam, as it is commonly called, is an importation from China, Japan and other countries of the Far East. It is like a large inverted brass pan, or perhaps a bronze pan. Its tonal effect is really awe-inspiring if used *fff* at the end of a climax, or when something sinister is meant to be depicted or suggested; when struck by a soft-headed drumstick, its tone is quite peculiar and strange, and fitting in characteristic compositions. It cannot be used for repeated notes, as the vibrations when once set in motion are difficult to control, and in consequence a curious jangle would result. It is notated for on one line.

EXAMPLES

See pages 227, 233.

The Castanets

French: *Castagnettes*
Italian: *Castagnette*
German: *Kastagnetten*

Spain and castanets are closely associated, although these clappers were introduced into Spain by the Moors. Castanets are somewhat similar in shape to two large halves of a brown hickory nut. They are clicked together by the fingers, each hand holding a pair. The newest castanets are not played in the original fashion, but are loosely attached to the end of a stick and "rattled." The various rhythms employed are quite typically Spanish in origin. One or two may aid the student.

EXAMPLES

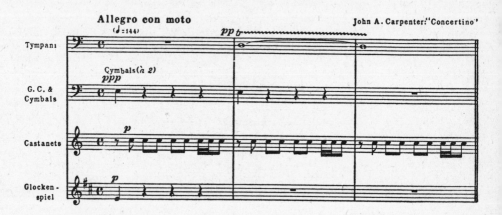

The Tenor Banjo   Plectrums

CHAPTER XXIII. THE TENOR BANJO; MANDOLIN; GUITAR; CYMBALON

THE TENOR BANJO

The banjo was formerly a solo instrument, or, which is perhaps more nearly correct, an accompanying instrument. It had five strings, four long and one short, and was the favorite medium of the negro in expressing his own peculiar style of music. From it he drew forth his original rhythms as well as his characteristic harmonizations.

The banjo is naturally rhythmic rather than melodic, and for this reason it has grooved itself into the modern dance or jazz orchestra as a means of stimulation and background.

Through a series of evolutions, it was found best for orchestral purposes to eliminate one of the strings. The short string, being the least essential, was removed. Various tunings for the remaining four strings were essayed, until at present the viola-tuning is adopted. It is no longer plucked with the fingers, for the exigencies of its orchestral uses necessitate a change of tone production, and the plectrum style has resulted.

The plectrum is a flexible pick, the same as is used in playing the mandolin, which makes it possible for the performer to derive a sustained tremolo tone as well as a more certain three or four note chord expression. It also gives to the instrument a greater volume of tone in solo passages and ensemble uses.

This orchestral banjo, or as it is now called *tenor banjo*, is a transposing instrument, sounding an octave lower than notated. Consequently all music to be played must be written an octave higher than it is intended to sound.

A peculiar system of notation is in vogue, in that the player forms or distributes the notes of the chord he is to play according to the note found in the melody. For example:

It will be seen, in this system of notation, that the arrangement of the notes of the chord is left entirely to the discretion of the player, who will distribute the factors of each chord according to the convenience of fingering, which depends upon the position of the fingers over the frets.

This way may be used for simple orchestral compositions of dance or jazz music where only rhythm and noise predominate; but for a more serious adaptation the actual notes of the chord, arpeggio or melody, should be written an octave higher, and this fact specifies that the part is to be played as notated.

In order to write a banjo part correctly, the fingering of the instrument should be carefully studied with a view to eliminating any awkwardness in the shifting of the hand over the frets.

Three or four note chords are playable in fast or slow tempo if the correct positions are maintained. When it is necessary to change positions, the chart of the finger board should be carefully studied and the chord involved so arranged as to move into the nearest available position.

THE MANDOLIN

French: *Mandoline*
Italian: *Mandolino*
German: *Mandoline*

While the mandolin is not an orchestral instrument, it is occasionally requisitioned for use in the orchestra for a special effect. Its double strings are tuned the same as the violin: G, D, A and E.

The fingering, which is the same as the violin, is indicated by frets inlaid in the finger board. The strings are of wire and set into vibration by means of a plectrum, or pick, of tortoise shell or celluloid held firmly between the thumb and fingers of the right hand.

Sustained notes are produced by quickly vibrating the pick across the two strings. Melodies containing notes of short time-value are more natural for the instrument than are sustained tones, although these are all playable in the tremolo-tenuto fashion described. No indication is necessary for these notes, as the performer will always sustain them their exact time-value. Chords are playable as on the violin, the fingering of all the stops being identical.

The practical range of the mandolin is

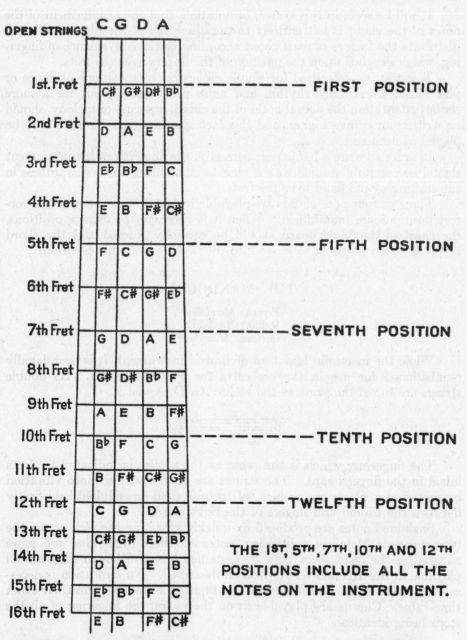

OPEN STRINGS	C	G	D	A
1st. Fret	C#	G#	D#	Bb
2nd Fret	D	A	E	B
3rd Fret	Eb	Bb	F	C
4th Fret	E	B	F#	C#
5th Fret	F	C	G	D
6th Fret	F#	C#	G#	Eb
7th Fret	G	D	A	E
8th Fret	G#	D#	Bb	F
9th Fret	A	E	B	F#
10th Fret	Bb	F	C	G
11th Fret	B	F#	C#	G#
12th Fret	C	G	D	A
13th Fret	C#	G#	Eb	Bb
14th Fret	D	A	E	B
15th Fret	Eb	Bb	F	C
16th Fret	E	B	F#	C#

FIRST POSITION

FIFTH POSITION

SEVENTH POSITION

TENTH POSITION

TWELFTH POSITION

THE 1ST, 5TH, 7TH, 10TH AND 12TH POSITIONS INCLUDE ALL THE NOTES ON THE INSTRUMENT.

BANJO FINGERBOARD WITH VIOLA TUNING.

THE GUITAR

French: *Guitare*
Italian: *Chitarra*
German: *Guitarre*

The guitar has been used to better advantage in the orchestra than has the mandolin, although neither instrument belongs to the orchestral body as an ensemble factor. The guitar is purely an accompanying instrument capable of performing chords or arpeggios across its six strings.

These are tuned:

Music for the guitar is written on the treble clef, but sounds an octave lower and consequently the range of the instrument is sounding

Harmonics are possible, but only effective in solo use. Repeated chords of from three to six notes are commonly employed, and these are often formed by placing one finger across several strings at the same point on the fretted finger board. These are called barré chords. As an accompanying instrument to the mandolin or to the strings the guitar finds its greatest instrumental use. As an accompaniment for the voice its rolled chords and arpeggios give a sustaining harmonic body quite appropriate in characteristic compositions.

The guitar has been used quite frequently in mixed orchestral and vocal scores. This combination is found in *The Barber*, by Rossini; *Oberon*, by Weber; and in the choral work, *Father and Daughter*, by Percy A. Grainger.

EXAMPLES

Olcott-Bickford: "Carry Me Back To Old Virginny"

Courtesy of Oliver Ditson Co.

Guitar Harmonics.

The Mandolin   The Guitar

THE CIMBALON OR DULCIMER

The cimbalon is Hungarian in origin, and is used a great deal in the Gypsy bands as an accompanying instrument. Its strings are tuned chromatically and are set in vibration by two wooden or soft-headed hammers. The instrument, which resembles the old-fashioned harpsichord without the keyboard or cover, has a range of four octaves and is

notated for on both the bass and treble clefs.

Chords are not possible, and consequently arpeggios of chord formation are substituted. The experienced cimbalon player performs these on his instrument in an astonishingly proficient manner, and in a tempo that ordinarily would seem impossible. Most of the music that one hears played by a Magyar performer is purely improvisation.

Sustained notes are produced in tremolo-tenuto by the use of the two hammers, and all varieties of tonal gradations are possible, though the instrument cannot be heard unless the accompaniment be reduced to a minimum.

CHAPTER XXIV. COMBINATION OF STRINGS, WOOD-WINDS, BRASSES AND PERCUSSIONS

The possible combinations of the strings, wood-winds, brasses and percussions are so numerous as to become almost entirely a matter of individual choice on the part of the composer.

The following combinations may be considered typical:

Small Orchestra

1 flute.	Percussions.
1 oboe.	First violins, 2 to 4.
2 clarinets.	Second violins, 2 or 3.
1 bassoon.	Violas, 1 or 2.
2 horns.	Violoncello, 1 or 2.
1 trumpet.	Double-bass, 1.
1 trombone.	

Medium-sized Orchestra

2 flutes.	Tuba.
2 oboes.	Percussions.
2 clarinets.	First violins, 4 to 8.
2 bassoons.	Second violins, 3 to 6.
2 to 4 horns.	Violas, 2 to 4.
2 trumpets.	Cellos, 2 to 4.
2 trombones.	Basses, 2.

Large Orchestra

3 flutes, third flute interchangeable with piccolo.	3 trombones.
	1 tuba.
2 oboes.	Percussions.
1 English horn.	Harp, 1 or 2.
2 or 3 clarinets.	First violins, 10 to 18 or more.
1 bass clarinet.	Second violins, 10 to 16 or more.
2 or 3 bassoons.	Violas, 8 to 12 or more.
1 double-bassoon.	Cellos, 8 to 12.
4 horns.	Basses, 6 to 10.
2 or 3 trumpets.	

These three combinations may be varied somewhat as to the number of instruments called for in the various choirs. In the small orchestra the oboe and bassoon may be omitted. In the medium-sized orchestra one oboe and one trumpet may suffice. The harp may also be used with this combination. In the large orchestra a great many variations will be found on studying the scores of the well-known orchestral writers.

The student is advised to watch the doubling of voices, both in unison and in the octave, the handling of the strings in combination with the wood-wind and brass choirs, the dynamic nuances, the entrances of the different groups, the contrasts in transference, etc.

The orchestral scores of the following composers should be carefully studied by the student, with a view to gaining a technical knowledge of the uses of the individual instruments as well as of the groupings in ensemble.

European Composers	*American Composers*
Beethoven:	G. W Chadwick.
Overtures, Symphonies.	Frederick A. Stock.
Berlioz.	John A. Carpenter.
Tschaikowsky:	Ch. M. Loeffler.
Symphonies.	Frederick S. Converse.
Rimsky-Korsakoff:	Eric De Lamarter.
Miscellaneous works.	Henry Hadley.
Wagner.	Leo Sowerby
Franck:	Ernest Bloch.
Symphony.	Arthur Shepherd.
Richard Strauss.	Emerson Whithorne.
d'Indy:	Victor Herbert.
Symphonies and orchestral excerpts.	Edgar Stillman Kelley.
Reger.	Howard Hanson.
String quartets.	Louis Adolphe Coerne.
Grieg	

And others of note, including the so-called " advanced " school.

Large Orchestra

One of the hardest tasks that the student of orchestration has before him is the combining of all the instruments of the orchestra, preserving a normal and natural balance of tonal distribution. In considering his tone-colors, he should classify the homogeneous instruments, such as the oboes, bassoons and double-bassoons; the clarinets and bass clarinet; the flutes and piccolo; the four horns; the trumpets, trombones and tuba; and the strings; assigning them their duties as to groupings rather than as careless, haphazard doublings. Keep the brasses, by which we mean trumpets, trombones and tuba, as a distinct harmonic choir, playing rather dispersed and full harmonization in the tutti passages. The trumpets may project the melody, with the trombones assisting an octave lower. In this case the horns may fill in the harmonies; but in all cases the brasses should solidify the massed tonal effect, giving body and strength harmonically as well as rhythmically.

When the brasses are storming forth the melody, the flutes and piccolo as well as the oboe and clarinet may also be doubling the melody in the highest register, thus permitting the highest strings to carry an ornamental figuration in conjunction with filled voices and counter-melodies in such instruments as second oboe, English horn, second clarinet, bassoons, etc.

In a climax, such orchestration is forcefully exhilarating, commanding attention and stimulating excitement through the rhythmic and tonal effects obtained. In all *tutti* passages the student should be careful to have the harmonic balance well distributed over the various choirs. In other words, the harmonies should not all be in the ponderous instruments at the bottom with a casual filling in of the weaker instruments in the middle, and the brilliant voices of the orchestra at the top. The student should carefully guard against overshadowing his theme, which matter may be facilitated by having it sufficiently doubled in the top voices of each choir. Each choir should be as complete harmonically as possible in a *tutti* The student is warned against "all top and bottom and no middle."

When the melody is being carried by a medium-pitched voice, such as the viola, a number of middle-registered instruments will be required to strengthen the melody by doubling in order that the brighter and also the heavier instruments will not entirely obliterate it. These accompanying instruments should be modified in tone-coloring in order to permit the weaker melody-carrying instruments to assert themselves.

In considering full orchestra, we do not expect *tutti* passages to continue throughout the composition. The main choir in the orchestra is the string section. As a whole, the strings are powerful if pitted against other individual voices such as a flute or a clarinet, almost entirely submerging either tone-color. Consequently an individual wood-wind should not be expected to carry the melody against a full body of strings, especially in *f* or *ff* passages. In such a case the strings should be subordinated in tone-color or, which is still better, the wood-wind carrying the melody should be strengthened by reinforcement of other like instruments.

The brasses are the most powerful voices of the orchestra. They dominate all else on the slightest occasion, and should be most rigidly held in place, not alone by order of tonal diminution, but also by unassertiveness of rhythm. Only when they are required to be powerfully predominating, both rhythmically and melodically, should they be permitted to do other than double in the non-essential chord-tones, in order to assemble background or to strengthen secondary melodic lines. This does not mean that they should overdo in the doubling of inner voices, as this always results in muddiness. Where rhythmic impetus is desired they may be unleashed, and they will discover themselves to be the centre of attention of the conductor as well as of the audience. The watchword

for their use is, *care*. When we speak of the brasses, we of course asso-
ciate the horns in this family; but we exempt them in the general rules
for the trumpets, trombones and tuba, for, as was mentioned in the chapter
on horns, they are neither brass nor wood-wind in quality. Consequently,
their adaptability in blending with all orchestral instruments is so great
as to make them very important and of great service. The horns are
wonderful harmonic instruments, giving body to the middle of the orchestral range. They can be regulated to suit any desired tonal picture and
still be background or foreground in the mood, at the will of the composer.

In planning a *tutti* for full orchestra, the student would do well to
arrange his strings in a more widely separate compass than he usually does
under ordinary circumstances, then fill in with wood-winds, horns and
brasses. But it is not to be supposed that the strings are to play the
extreme outer parts and the rest of the orchestra the middle; it is
desirable to have the warmth of the strings distributed throughout the
entire orchestral compass. The strings then fit in well with the dispersed
harmonies of the brasses, doubling with the horns and wood-winds and
intermingling more successfully than if they were confined to only a
portion of the compass. This we call *balance;* and it is only through
such consideration of groupings that the best effects in orchestration are
obtainable.

When the strings and brasses are properly balanced, the matter of
adjusting the wood-winds becomes comparatively simple; for in *tutti*, the
two predominating choirs, strings and brasses, will in most instances over-
power the rest of the orchestra. The wood-winds will then be used for
doubling, filling in and ornamenting. It is in such spots as these that we
find the piccolo boastingly soaring above the other voices in trills, runs
and occasional spurts of melody. It is also here that we find the percussions in more deliberate rhythmic delineation than elsewhere; but with all,
the strings and brasses continue to monopolize and propel the most important phases of the orchestral song, especially the strings, which, after
all, constitute the backbone of the orchestral choirs.

In these days, when orchestral effects are so varied through the uses
of instruments which did not exist in the days of Beethoven and his con-
temporaries, new inventions are daily being brought forward. It is difficult to keep up with the modern tendencies, for what was once considered
irrational or unusual in tonal effect no longer draws our particular attention
or excites comment. Our duty, however, is to begin rationally, and, after
feeling a firm foundation under our feet, then to essay experimentation
in orchestral painting, individual to our expression.

The orchestral composer has many combinations for which to write.
He does not always need an orchestra of unusual proportions. Odd com-

binations are occasionally used, besides ensembles of wood-winds, or wood-winds and brasses combined, or strings and wood-winds, etc. A notable ensemble, which in its way was most astonishingly proficient and gratifying, was the body of artists called the Barrère Ensemble, comprised principally of wood-winds and horns. The number of compositions for such a combination was entirely adequate to permit of a series of concerts each year, exhibiting variety of effect and arousing a wide and decidedly keen interest in musical circles.

Barrere Ensemble

CHAPTER XXV. SUGGESTIONS FOR COPYING ORCHESTRAL PARTS

In the copying of orchestral parts, the composer should see to it that no details are lacking that will be of material aid to the performers. Parts which are carefully written in generous sized notes with no doubts as to whether they are on lines or spaces and which have the stems, etc., in their proper places, invite a deeper interest on the part of the players than would carelessly written parts. In attending rehearsals of large symphony orchestras, where time cannot be granted for minute scrutiny of orchestral parts and comparisons with the score, we have often noted the complete lack of interest on the part of the men in the orchestra when parts are given them to perform that are badly copied and barren of the necessary indications of tempi, nuance, expressions, cues, and the general information that the routined performers expect.

An orchestral performer should not be required to take anything for granted, even though he is expected to be an experienced performer on his instrument; for not only must he intuitively follow the conductor's beat, but also his interpretative demands. Beside these important considerations, the player is reading at sight, and his work should be facilitated in every possible way. Any little aid given him will bear fruit in the result obtained, and be most gratifying to the composer.

In the first place, the composer should check up carefully on all the transposing instruments employed and see to it that the "sour notes," as the orchestra men call them, are eliminated. His next duty is to go through the entire score and letter or number it at convenient intervals in order that the conductor may rehearse fragments, when necessary, without having to count back measures to find a convenient point for all to start. These letters or numbers should be generously distributed, preferably in colored pencil and framed in a square or circle.

His next consideration in regard to the copying of parts (and this is of great importance) is the matter of "cuing." He cannot be too generous in this respect, for the performer not only expects this aid, he demands it, especially in passages where the melody overlaps from one instrument into another. After a pause of a half dozen measures in a part, one measure

201

of the melody being played by another instrument should be cued in with the name of the instrument performing as well as the expression to be employed. Thus:

After a long pause it is well to cue in two or three measures:

When two instrumental voices are duetting, it is well to have both voices indicated throughout the parts of both performers in order that they may be more definitely in sympathy with each other.

A cued-in melody, here and there, during a lengthy inactivity on the part of a rarely employed instrument, is greatly appreciated by the performer. It not only lightens his burden of keeping accurate count of the measures, but keeps him in more intimate touch with the music.

Another assistance which is greatly appreciated by the orchestra is the liberal sized note on a not too narrow staff. Do not crowd! Take plenty of space and use *black* ink — *never blue!* Watch, in the copying of parts, that the turning of the page is at a convenient point in the music. Economy of paper in such matters is a poor policy to follow. It is much better to spread out notes than to cramp them into illegibility. Number pages carefully, with the title of the composition and the composer's name on each page, in case they become misplaced or mixed with other parts on the stands. This detail will be appreciated by the librarian whose duty it is to keep things in order and ready for performance at a moment's notice.

A well-known conductor once related an incident apropos of this matter. He found a manuscript score on his office desk which bore neither the composer's name nor a title on any portion of it. On examining the work he discovered it worthy of performance; but knowing neither the author's name nor what to call it, he was obliged to file it away to await developments, thinking that the composer would return for a verdict on its musical value. It had been shelved for ten years at the time that the author of this volume was going through the well-stocked library of scores, and in the interim no inkling of who had written the inspired work had reached headquarters. It could not be performed, as the conductor did not know to whom he should attribute authorship; neither could he program it, for it bore no title. And there it rests in silence because of the modesty or carelessness of the composer.

Copy parts for each instrument in the orchestra, except for the strings. Here one part suffices for each two instruments of the same type. By no means attempt to copy two parts, such as for two flutes or two clarinets, etc., on one staff. Each performer must have his own part with ample cues, especially when he is performing an intricate, antiphonal duet or other florid passage.

In cuing for the heavier instruments of the orchestra, such as the trumpets, horns, trombones, etc., be sure to select passages for cues which can be heard, and not obscure passages on instruments which are easily "buried" by the more assertive orchestral voices.

In the matter of leger lines above and below the staff be sure that the spaces between such added lines are equal to the spaces on the printed staff. Do not crowd leger lines together, especially in flute parts or high string passages, as carelessness in this matter is extremely annoying to the performer.

These fine points concerning the copying of score into orchestral parts, while seemingly naïve and to be expected of the composer, are very often overlooked. As has already been stated at different times throughout this work, details should never be neglected. One cannot be too explicit or too careful, for the composer's duty does not stop with the birth of an idea. This attention to detail should continue religiously throughout the entire growth of his work until it is thoroughly prepared for artistic rendition.

CHAPTER XXVI. MUSICAL TERMS, EXPRESSIONS AND INDICATIONS USED BY ORCHESTRAL COMPOSERS

The conductors and instrumental performers of to-day must be either linguists or exceptionally good guessers in order to follow the directions found in the orchestral scores or parts which they are called upon to interpret. Upon examining scores by American, French, German, Italian, Russian, Spanish and English composers, we find that each employs certain markings in abbreviated Italian, such as *p, pp, f, ff, sfz, mf, sf*, etc., and then placidly uses his own native tongue or the German language for all further directions. Some composers use a great detail of expression marks, others barely enough to indicate the rate of speed to be taken and the general tone-color desired. Some help the conductor and performers by a stimulative word here and there disclosing the imaginative mood to be depicted. Then, again, we find the composer with an exceptional knowledge of each instrument bridging over difficulties by explicit instructions as to tunings, changes, positions and helpful suggestions which at once win the admiration and esteem of the entire orchestral body.

What advice shall be given the American composer other than to follow the natural trend of the times and employ the commonly used Italian abbreviations, supplementing these with his own language for further directions? Why should we not take it upon ourselves to expect musicians of foreign nationalities to interpret and understand our language just as they expect others to understand theirs? Taking it for granted that compositions by Americans will be more frequently performed by American orchestras than by orchestras of foreign countries, there is no reason why the native composer should be hampered in expressing himself by being obliged to use a language with which, ninety-nine times out of a hundred, he is unfamiliar. He spends time and energy in making necessary translations when he employs a language other than his own; and even then if he is not acquainted with the flexibilities and idioms of the tongue in which he is endeavoring to express himself, his directions are not as concise and thorough as they should be.

The composer owes it to his art to make himself as intelligible and forceful in his expression as it is possible to be, and he should exhibit no qualms in expressing his desires as regards performance of his work in the language with which he is most familiar.

The short tables of musical terminology which are presented herewith are solely for the purpose of aiding the student in score reading, and not for use in his own composing unless he so desires.

These terms were taken from the scores of French, German, Italian,

English and American composers, and are by no means to be considered as in any way complete lists of all the expressions commonly used. The table of English terms is added as suggestive of the way in which our own language may be utilized in giving proper directions in the scoring for orchestra.

The following terms were found in the scores of Claude Achille Debussy and François Poulence:

French Musical Terminology

Archet — bow.
Assez uniform — quite uniform.
Au mouvt. — in original tempo.
Bagnettes de timbales — drumsticks.
Cédez — slow up.
Comme un léger bruissement — lightly rustling.
Comme un coup de sifflet — like a whistled tone.
De la pointe — with the point of the bow.
Doux et flottant — sweet and floating, gently and lightly.
Doux et léger — sweet and light.
En dehors — to the front, in evidence.
En diminuant presque plus rien — diminish to almost silence.
En laissant vibrer — let vibrate naturally.
Express. — expressive.
Gaiment — gayly.
Glissando tres mesuré — even, measured, glissando.
Gracieux — gracious.
Le chant en dehors — the melody in evidence.
Le double plus lent — twice as slow.
Légère — lightly, nimbly, softly.
Léger — lightly, nimbly, softly.
Légèrement — still softer or lighter.
Mailloche de grosse caisse — bass drumstick.
Marqué — marked rhythm.
Modéré — moderate.
Modérément animé — moderately fast and spirited.
Ôtez — remove.
Ôtez la Sourdine — remove mute.
Peu — a little, a trifle.
Peu plus — a little more (referring to expressions such as *p, pp, f,* etc.).
Plus — more.
Plus assoupli — dying away, diminishing.
Près de la table — near the sounding board (for the harp).
Près du chevalet — near the bridge.
I.ers de chaque pupitre — the firsts at each stand.
Reprenez la Gde Fl. — change back from piccolo to flute.
Retenu — hold back slightly, same as rit. or rall.
Sec — dry.
Sons bouchés — muted notes of horn.
Sons cuivrés — brassy notes of horn.
Sons d'echo — echo sounds of horn.

Sur la touche — on the finger board.
Sourdine — mute.
Tous — all together.
Très court — very short.
Très en dehors — very much in evidence.
Très soutenir — very sustained.
Très vite — very fast.
Unis — together.
Un peu cédé — a bit slower.
Un peu plus movementé — a little faster.

Italian Musical Terminology

Accellerando, accel., acc., — faster.
Affretando — hurrying. Affretoso — hurried.
Allargando — growing broader and slightly slower.
Alquanto lento — with exacting slowness.
Animato — animated.
Aperto — open.
Appasionato — with passion, emotionally, ardently.
Attacca — begin the next.
Bacchetta — stick.
Calando — decreasing in loudness.
Chiuso — closed, stopped.
Con fuoco — with fire, energy, force.
Con passione — with passion.
Con la bacchetta — with drumstick.
Con la mazza — with bass drumstick.
Come prima ma un poco tranquillo — as at the beginning, but more tranquil.
Dolce — sweet.
Dolciss. — sweetly.
Doloroso — sadly.
Espress, Espr. — with expression.
Force un poco piu presto — perhaps a trifle faster.
Forza — force, energy.
Fiati — wood-winds.
Fuoco — fire.
Giusto — exact, strict, precise.
Grandioso — pompous or in grand style.
Grazioso — graceful.
Largamente — largely, broadly.
Leggermente mosso — lightly moving.
Lento — slowly.
Lunga — long hold.
Maestoso — majestically.
Marcato, Marc. — emphatic.
Marcatissimo — very emphatic.
Mazza — bass drumstick.
Meno mosso — less movement, less impelled.
Metà — the half.
Moderato assai — quite a moderate speed, including intensity.

Molto pesante — very ponderous, heavy.
Molto rall. — much slower.
Molto rallent — much slower.
Molto rubato e grazioso — impassionedly sentimental and graceful.
Morendo — dying out.
Mormorando — murmuring, subdued.
Mormoroso — murmuring, subdued.
Muta — change.
Muta in piccolo — change to piccolo.
Muta in A — referring to trumpet or clarinet.
Naturale — unaffected.
Nobilmente e semplice — with noble simplicity.
Oscillante — vibrating.
Ottavino, Ott. — piccolo.
Pesante — heavy, ponderous.
Poco accel. — a trifle faster.
Poco animato — slightly more animated.
Poco a poco — gradually.
Poco meno mosso — a little less movement.
Ponticello — near the bridge, effecting a strident sound.
Poco piu moso — a little more movement.
Portando — slow glissando.
Più — more.
Più P — softer.
Più F — louder.
Scherzando — playful, humorous, sportive.
Sempre — always.
Sempre P — always soft.
Sensible — naturally.
Senza — without.
Senza colore — without color.
Simile — in like manner, the same.
Sonoramente — very sonorous.
Sonoro — sonorously.
String. poco a poco — gradually quickening.
Stringendo — accelerating, hastening.
Sordino — mute.
Sostenuto, sost. — sustained.
Subito — suddenly, quickly.   F subito P.
Sulla tastiera — on the finger board.
Teneramente — tenderly, delicately, equivalent to dolce.
Tenuto, Ten. — held a trifle, or given full-time value.
Tranquillo — quietly, tranquilly.
Tutti — together or all together.
Tutta forza — with full force.
Un, Una — one.
Uniti — united, together.
Via sordina — remove the mute.
Vibrato — wavering effect.

German Musical Terminology

Abnehmen — diminish.
Abschwellen — decrease.
Abstossen — staccato.
Anschwellen — increase in loudness.
Aufführung — performance.
Aufgeweckt — lively.
Bassposaune — bass trombone.
Bass-schlüssel — bass clef.
Bebung — tremolo.
Becken — cymbals.
Bedeckt — stopped.
Begeisterung — spirit, enthusiasm.
Bémol — B flat.
Bes — B double-flat.
Blechinstrument — brass instrument.
Bogen — bow.
Bratsche — viola.
Breit — broad, stately, slowly.
Chor — combination of instruments of same family.
Dämpfer — mute.
Des — D flat.
Dis — D sharp.
Doppel — double.   Doppelfagott, etc.
Drängend — pressing, hastening.
Durchführung — development.
Eilen — to hasten, accelerate.
Eilend — hurrying.
Eilig — swift.
Ein, Eins — one.
Einfach — simple.
Eingang — introduction, prelude.
Einleitung — introduction, prelude.
Eis — E sharp.
Ergriffen — affected, stirred, agitated.
Erster, Erste, Erstes — first.
Es — E flat.
Etwas — rather, somewhat.
Fagott — bassoon.
Fein — delicate, fine.
Fes — F flat.
Fest. — I, a festival;   II, firm, steady.
Feuer — fire, ardor.
Feuerig — fiery, passionately.
Fis — F sharp.
Fisis — F double-sharp.
Fuss — foot.
Frei — freely.
Ganz — whole, very.
Gebrochen — broken.

Gedämpft — muffled, muted.
Gefühl — feeling.
Geige — violin.
Geist — soul, spirit.
Geistlich — sacred.
Geläufig — fluent, easy.
Gelassen — calm, placid.
Gemächlich — comfortable.
Gemässigt — moderate.
Gemüth — soul, heart, spirit.
Gerade — similar.
Ges — G flat.
Geses — G double-flat.
Getheilt — divided.
Getragen — sustained.
Glocke — bell.
Griffbrett — finger board.
Gut — good.
Heftig — impetuous, vehement.
Heiter — serene, cheerful.
Holzbläser — wood-winds.
Immer — always, as; immer starker werdend, **etc.**
Innig — heartfelt, sincere.
Inständig — urgent, pressing.
Kadenz — cadence, close.
Kammermusik — chamber music.
Kapellmeister — conductor.
Kastagnetten — castanets.
Keck — bold, pert.
Klang — sound.
Klangboden — sound board.
Klangfarbe — tone-color.
Klarinette — clarinet.
Klingend — sounding.
Kontrabass — double-bass.
Kraft — force, vigor.
Kräftig — forceful, vigorous.
Kreischend — harsh, strident.
Kurz — short, crisp.
Lage — position.
Langsam — slowly.
Langsamer — slower.
Launig — gayly.
Laut — loud.
Lebendig — lively.
Lebhaft — lively.
Leise — soft.
Lieblich — sweetly, lovely, charming.
Lied — song.
Lustig — merry, gay.

Mässig — moderate.
Mehr — more.
Mit — with.
Niederschlag — down beat.
Noch — still, yet.
Ober — higher.
Oder — or, or else.
Offen — open.
Offenbar — open.
Pause — rest.
Posaune — trombone.
Prächtig — splendid, grand.
Rauh — harsh, rough, hoarse.
Rhythmus — rhythm.
Rückgang — repetition.
Ruhig — quiet, tranquil, calm.
Saite — string.
Saiteninstrumente — string instruments.
Sanft — soft.
Shaurig — expression of mortal dread or terror.
Schluss — close, end, cadence.
Schlusskadenz — closing cadence.
Schlusssatz — finale.
Schwer — heavy, hard, ponderous.
Schwermütig — melancholy, sad.
Schwindend — dying away.
Schwungvoll — with sweep and passion.
Sehnsucht — yearning, longing.
Sehr — very.
Spiel — play.
Ständchen — serenade.
Stark — loud.
Stärker — louder.
Steg — bridge.
Sterbend — dying out.
Stimme — voice.
Stimmungsvoll — full of expression.
Stopfen — to stop or mute the horn with the hand.
Stopftöne — stopped tones.
Streichorchester — string orchestra.
Streng — strict, severe.
Stück — a piece or number.
Stürmish — stormy, impetuous.
Süess — sweet.
Takt — beat.
Taktmässig — keeping time.
Im takt — a tempo.
Traurig — sadly.
Trommel — drum.
Trübe — gloomy, dismal, sad.

Uber — above, over.
Unruhig — restless, nervous.
Unter — under, below.
Ventilhorn — valve-horn.
Viel — much, great.
Mit vielen Nachdruck — with strong emphasis.
Voll — full.
Volles Orchester — full orchestra.
Vom — from.
Vom Anfang — from the beginning.
Wärme — warmth, ardor.
Mit grosser Wärme — with great warmth.
Weich — tender.
Wehmuth — sadness.
Weit — broad.
Wenig — little.
Ein klein wenig langsamer — a trifle slower.
Wie — as.
Wie vorher — as before.
Wieder — again.
Wuchtig — heavy.
Würde — dignity.
Mit Würde — with dignity.
Wuthend — furious, frantic.
Zart — tender.
Zartlich — caressingly.
Zeit — time.
Zeitness — tempo.
Ziemlich — somewhat, rather.
Zierlich — delicate, graceful.
Zinke — cornet.
Zitternd — trembling.
Zögernd — hesitating or lingering.
Zünge — tongue.
Zurückhalten — hold back, retard.
Zusammen — together.

English Musical Terminology

Above.
Accelerating.
Accented.
Altogether.
Ardently.
Bowed.
Brassy.
Breezily.
Brightly.
Bring out the melody.
Briskly.
Broadly, broader.

Brusque.
Calm.
Cheerfully, cheerful.
Change to piccolo or flute or to A clarinet or bass clarinet.
Charmingly.
Decidedly (forceful, fervent, passionate, etc.).
Decreasing (in tempo, in loudness).
Drumsticks.
Delicately.
Defined.
Dry.
Dully.
Easily.
Echo.
Elegant.
Emphatic.
Expressive.
Fast, faster.
Fervently.
Fiery.
Firsts at each stand.
Floating.
Flowingly.
Forcefully.
Forcefully decisive, etc.
Gayly.
Gently.
Gloriously.
Gracious.
Grandly.
Greatly retarded.
Humorously.
Hurry, hurried, hurrying.
Impulsive.
In a jocose manner.
Increasing in time (in loudness).
In grand manner or style.
Intensely.
In time.
In quiet mood.
Jocose.
Jokingly.
Lingering.
Long pause.
Loud, louder, loudly.
Melodiously.
Mellow.
Moderately (fast, slow, loud, soft, etc.).
Mute, muted.
Near bridge.

Nervously.
Nimbly.
Noisy, noisily.
Original tempo.
Passionately.
Pick up speed.
Playful.
Plucked.
Pointedly.
Ponderous.
Pompously.
Precise.
Pressing.
Put on mute.
Quick.
Quiet.
Quietly, very quiet.
Querulously.
Rather (quiet, loud, sweet, short, etc.).
Reasonably (fast, slow, loud, soft, etc.).
Rest.
Retard.
Ringing.
Rollicking.
Rousing.
Similar.
Simply, simplicity.
Slacken speed.
Slide up; slide down.
Slightly (softer, louder, broader, thinner, etc.).
Slow up (slightly, quietly, quickly, carefully, easily, etc.).
Slowly, slower, slowing up.
Soft.
Sonorously.
Snappy.
Speedily.
Stridently.
Supplicatingly.
Steadily.
Sustained.
Take piccolo again.
Together.
Take off mute.
Tip of bow.
Vibrate.
Vividly.
Warmly.
With noble simplicity.

from "Concert Overture in C Major" (with Organ)

ARTHUR EDWARD JOHNSTONE

from "Comes Autumn Time"

Animato e giogoso   LEO SOWERBY

Deuxieme Symphonie

VINCENT d'INDY

Chromatic passage work in horns.

from "C minor Symphony"

FRIED. A. STOCK

"Dirge" from Concerto Grosso

ERNEST BLOCH

from "Flivver Ten Million"
FREDERICK S. CONVERSE

from "Forest Spirits"
Suite for large orchestra

EDWARD A. MAC DOWELL

Courtesy of Arthur P. Schmidt

from "Il Finto Arlecchino"

G. FRANCESCO MALIPIERO

from "In Bohemia"

HENRY HADLEY

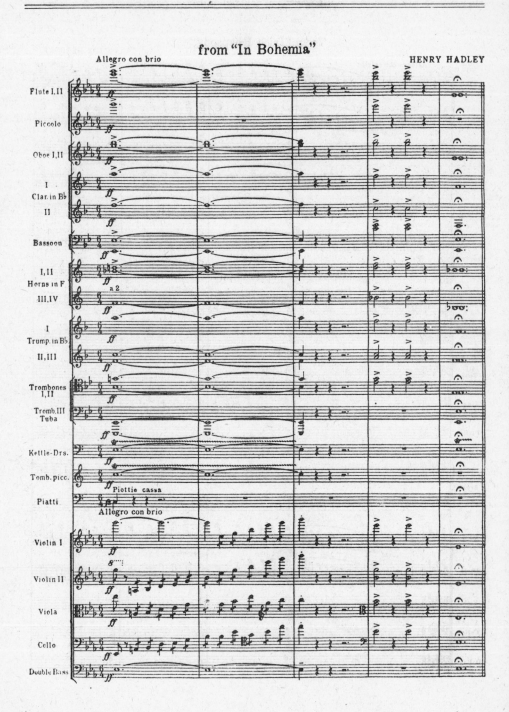

from "Irish Rhapsody"

VICTOR HERBERT

from "La Mort de Tintagiles"

CH. M. LOEFFLER

from "Legend Symphonique"

ERNEST SCHELLING

from "New England Symphony"

EDGAR STILLMAN-KELLEY

from "Piano Concerto" d minor

ARTHUR HINTON

from "Offrandes"
For Voice and Chamber Orchestra

EDGAR VARÈSE

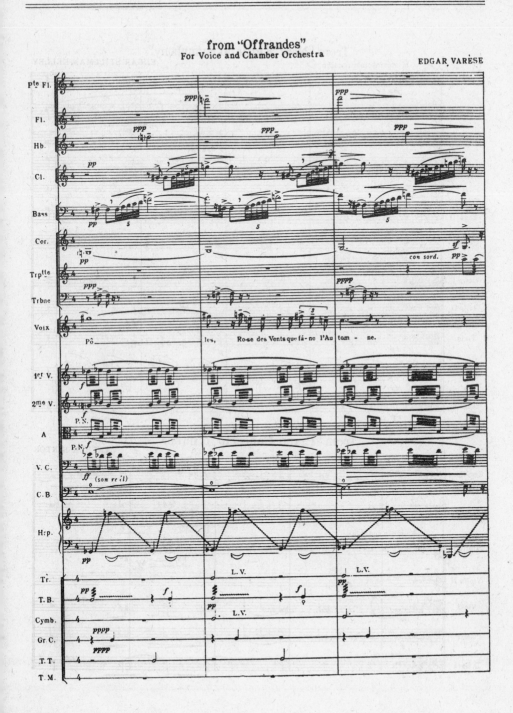

from "Overture to a Drama"

A. SHEPHERD

From PAN AND THE PRIEST

HOWARD HANSON, Op. 26

from "Peer Gynt Suite"

E. GRIEG

from "New Year's Eve In New York"
Symphonic Poem

WERNER JANSSEN

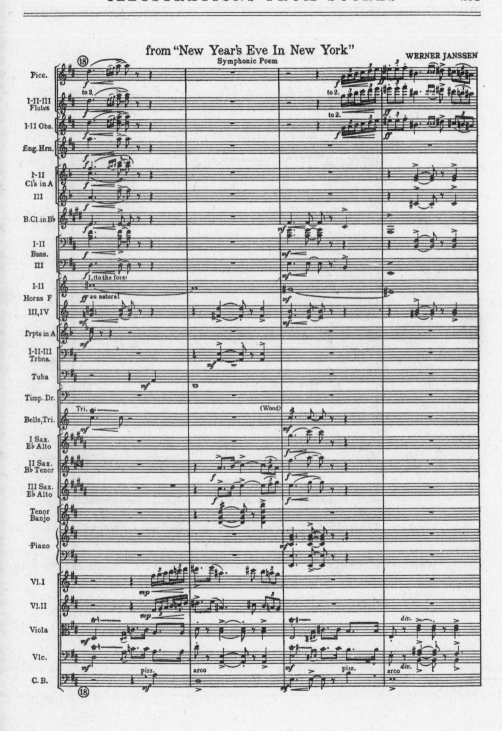

from "A Romantic Suite"

MAX REGER

from "Saturday's Child"
For Voices and Orchestra

Text by COUNTEE CULLEN

EMERSON WHITHORNE, Op. 42

from "2nd Symphony"

A. BORODIN

from "Sinfonietta"

G W CHADWICK

from "Soliloquy"
for Flute and String Orchestra

BERNARD ROGERS

OVERTURE
Wilhelm Tell

GIOACCHINO ROSSINI
1792-1868

An example of divisi cellos.

from Song Of The Volga Boatmen
A Choral Symphonic Paraphrase of an Old Russian Folk Song

ALBERT STOESSEL

from "Sonata"

PIETRO CASTRUCCI
Set for Strings by A. Walter Kramer

Danse de la Balerine
from Pétrouchka

d'IGOR STRAWINSKY

(Cornet-a-Pistons a la Main) Usually performed on a B♭ Trumpet.

Trumpet figuration.

Good Friday Spell
from Parsifal

RICHARD WAGNER
(1813-1883)

Bass choir of Horns, Trombones and low strings.

OVERTURE
La Grande Pâque Russe

N. RIMSKY-KORSAKOW. Op. 36

Trombones in unison.

V Polonaise
from Suite № 2, B minor

JOHANN SEBASTIAN BACH
(1685–1750)

Example of Flute figuration.

Ein Heldenleben

RICHARD STRAUSS, Op. 40

Wide expressive cantabile passages.

Scheherazade

N. RIMSKY-KORSAKOW, Op. 35

Woodwind Choir with Horns.

INDEX

Compositions are entered under the composer's name.
Numbers refer to pages.

Alto. *See* Viola.
Ambrosio, 24.

Banjo, 191.
Bantock, 110, 166, 174, 184.
Bass. *See* Double-Bass.
Bass Clarinet, 114.
Bass Drum, 181–182.
Bass Flute, 98.
Bass Trombone, 146, 148, 149.
Bass Tuba. *See* Tuba.
Bassoon, 117–120.
Beach, 96.
Beaters and Hammers:
    Cymbals, 188.
    Dulcimer, 195.
    Gong, 189.
    Kettledrums, 170.
    Snare Drum, 178.
    Xylophone, 177.
Beethoven, 25, 42, 119, 120, 136.
Bells. *See* Cathedral Chimes.
Bergé, 122, 189.
Borodine, 71.
Bowing:
    Double-Bass, 67.
    Viola, 44.
    Violin, 21, 34.
    Violoncello, 57.
Brahms, 17.
Brasses:
    Horns, 127.
    Trombones, 146.
    Trumpets, 139.
    Tuba, 153.
Burleigh, 37.
Busch, 45.

Cadman, 145.
Carillon. *See* Orchestra Bells.

Carpenter, 95, 112, 116, 120, 122, 137, 174, 184, 190.
Casella, 119.
Castanets, 189.
Celesta, 175–176.
Cello. *See* Violoncello.
Chabrier, 112.
Chadwick, 94, 110, 116, 142, 156.
Chalumeau, 108.
Chaminade-Kreisler, 31.
Chromatic Drums, 171.
Chromatic Harp, 165.
Cimbals. *See* Cymbals.
Clarinet in E♭, 113.
Clarinets in B♭ and A, 105–109.
Clementi, 86.
Combinations, Orchestral, 124, 196.
Contra-Bass. *See* Double-Bass.
Contra-Bassoon. *See* Double-Bassoon.
Converse, 70, 122, 151, 156, 186.
Copying Parts, 201.
Cor de Chasse, 127.
Cornets in B♭ and A, 144–145.
Cymbals, 187–189.

Dallam, 24, 74, 87, 137.
Debussy, 78, 101, 103, 122, 166, 168, 176, 184.
Delamarter, 73, 75, 76.
Delibes, 37, 101.
Delius, 72, 94, 167.
Détaché, 22.
Divisi. *See* String Orchestra.
Double-Bass:
    Bowing, 67.
    Fingering, 67.
    General, 66.
    Harmonics, 69.
Double-Bassoon, 121–122.

Drums:
    Bass Drum, 181.
    Chromatic Drum, 171.
    Kettledrums, 170.
    Snare Drum, 178.
Dukas, 75, 137.
Dulcimer, 195.

Elgar, 115, 155, 172, 180.
Elman, 40.
Embouchure, 133.
English Horn, 102–103.
Enharmonic Unisons, 163.
Euphonium, 153.
Exercises, 16, 23, 30, 46, 52, 60, 65, 71, 97,
    104, 116, 126, 138, 143, 152, 157.

Fagott. See Bassoon.
Finston, 142.
Flute, 91–92.
Flute, Bass, 98.
Franck, 17, 94, 103.
French Horn, 128–138.

Glazounow, 182, 184.
Glockenspiel. See Orchestra Bells.
Gong, 189.
Grainger, 72, 156, 178.
Granados, 122.
Griffes, 32, 51, 59, 64, 172, 189.
Guitar, 194.

Hadley, 104, 112, 116, 151, 156.
Harmonics:
    Double-Bass, 69.
    Harp, 163.
    Viola, 49.
    Viola d'Amore, 53.
    Violin, 29, 30.
    Violoncello, 62.
Harp, 161–168.
Herbert, 64, 151.
Holmes, 151.
Honegger, 119.
Horn, French, 128.
Horn, Hunting, 127.

Illustrations from scores, 214–245.
Indy, d', 17, 63, 86, 100, 111, 112, 120, 142,
    166, 172, 185.

Kettledrums, 169, 170–172.
Kettledrums, Chromatic, 171.
Kettledrums, Mechanical, 171.
Kolar, 172.

Lee, 58.
Legato, 21.
Liszt, 101.
Loeffler, 54, 103, 112, 115, 182.
Loomis, 97.

Mandolin, 192–193.
Marcato, 22.
Marimba, 178.
Mendelssohn, 23.
Meyerbeer, 136.
Molique, 58, 62.
Mozart, 42.
Mutes:
    Cornet, 144.
    Double-Bass, 77, 202.
    Harp, 164.
    Horn, 135.
    Trumpet, 141.
    Viola, 59, 77.
    Violin, 35, 77.
    Violoncello, 59, 77.

Oboe, 99, 100, 101.
Olcott-Bickford, 194.
Oldberg, 101, 103, 142, 150, 155.
Orchestra Bells, 173.

Paine, 94.
Parker, 45.
Piccolo, 92–93.
Pizzicato:
    Double-Bass, 69, 70.
    Violin, 35.
Ponticello, 45.
Powell, 176.

Rabaud, 136.
Rachmaninoff-Elman, 40.
Reger, 110, 138.
Rimsky-Korsakow, 110, 180.

Saint-Saëns, 32, 39, 101.
Sanford, 85, 86.
Sarasate, 40.

Sarrusophone, 159–160.
Saxophone, 158–159.
Schelling, 104, 122.
Sinding, 62.
Smetana, 150.
Smith, 63, 73, 174.
Snare Drum, 178–179.
Sowerby, 32, 40, 51, 59, 64, 76, 77, 95, 142, 143, 167, 168, 174, 176, 188.
Spalding, 31, 32, 38, 39.
Spiccato, 22.
Staccato, 22.
Stillman-Kelley, 58, 126, 155.
Stock, 17, 85, 95, 137, 138, 142.
Stopped Tones, 135, 164.
Stradivarius, 12.
Strauss, 100.
String Orchestra, 79.
Strings and Wood-Winds, 123.
Strube, 45, 150.

Tambourine, 183.
Tam-Tam. See Gong.
Taylor, 46, 51, 120, 122.
Tenor Banjo. See Banjo.
Timpani. See Kettledrums.
Tremolo-Legato, 34, 44, 77, 118.
Tremolo-Vibrato, 35, 44, 77.
Triangle 185–186.
Tromba. See Trumpet.
Trombone, 146–148.
Trombone, Bass, 148–149.
Trumpet, Bass, 143.
Tschaikowsky, 119.
Tuba, BB♭, 153.
Tuba, E♭, 153.
Tubular Bells, 173.

Valve-Trombone, 146.
Viola, 41.
    Bowing, 44.
    Double-Stops, 44.
    Fingering, 43.
    Harmonics, Artificial, 49.
    Harmonics, Natural 49.
    Other Stops, 48.
    Tone-Color, 50.
Viola d'Amore, 52.
    Harmonics, Artificial, 53.
    Harmonics, Natural, 53.
    Stops, 54.
    Tone-Color, 52–53.
Violin, 18.
    Bowing, 21, 34.
    Double-Stops, 18, 25, 26, 27, 28.
    Fingering, 19, 20, 27, 28.
    Harmonics, Artificial, 29, 30.
    Harmonics, Natural, 29.
    Stops, 18, 25, 26, 27, 28, 33, 34.
Violoncello, 55.
    Bowing, 57.
    Fingering, 56.
    Harmonics, Artificial, 62, 63.
    Harmonics, Natural, 62.
    Stops, 57, 61.
Vivaldi, 51, 78.

Wagner, 133.
Walker, 24, 31, 58.
Wier, 31.
Wind Ensemble, 196–200.
Wood-Wind Ensemble, 123–125.

Xylophone, 177.

Ysaÿe, 45, 151, 172.